The

HER CAMPUS℠

Guide to

COLLEGE LIFE

The HER CAMPUS℠

Guide to

COLLEGE LIFE

HOW TO MANAGE RELATIONSHIPS,
STAY SAFE AND HEALTHY,
HANDLE STRESS, AND HAVE
The Best Years of Your Life!

Stephanie Kaplan Lewis, Annie Chandler Wang,
Windsor Hanger Western, and the Writers & Editors of Her Campus

Avon, Massachusetts

Published by
Adams Media, a division of F+W Media, Inc.
57 Littlefield Street, Avon, MA 02322. U.S.A.
www.adamsmedia.com

ISBN 10: 1-4405-8511-3
ISBN 13: 978-1-4405-8511-1
eISBN 10: 1-4405-8512-1
eISBN 13: 978-1-4405-8512-8

Printed in the United States of America.

10 9 8 7 6 5 4 3 2 1

The information in this book should not be used for diagnosing or treating any health problem. Not all diet and exercise plans suit everyone. You should always consult a trained medical professional before starting a diet, taking any form of medication, or embarking on any fitness or weight-training program. The author and publisher disclaim any liability arising directly or indirectly from the use of this book.

Many of the designations used by manufacturers and sellers to distinguish their products are claimed as trademarks. Where those designations appear in this book and F+W Media, Inc. was aware of a trademark claim, the designations have been printed with initial capital letters. Collegiette is a registered trademark of Her Campus Media LLC.

This publication is designed to provide accurate and authoritative information with regard to the subject matter covered. It is sold with the understanding that the publisher is not engaged in rendering legal, accounting, or other professional advice. If legal advice or other expert assistance is required, the services of a competent professional person should be sought.
    —From a *Declaration of Principles* jointly adopted by a Committee of the
    American Bar Association and a Committee of Publishers and Associations

Cover design by Frank Rivera.

This book is available at quantity discounts for bulk purchases.
For information, please call 1-800-289-0963.

Dedication and Acknowledgments

We would like to thank our talented team of editors who put this book together: Alice Chen, Brittany Lewis, Michelle Lewis, Kate Moriarty, Cara Sprunk, Quinn Cohane, and Chelsea Evans, as well as our fabulous intern Elyssa Sternberg.

We would also like to acknowledge our incredible team of Her Campus contributing writers whose articles informed this book: Abby Feiner, Ainslie Forsum, Aja Frost, Alaine Perconti, Alex Gladu, Alexa Cleary, Alexandra Churchill, Alexis Benveniste, Ali Robertson, Alicia Thomas, Allie Jones, Allie Klein, Alyssa Grossman, Amanda First, Amanda Klohmann, Annie Pei, Annie Wazer, Aylin Erman, Becky McColl, Cameron Simcik, Carlene Helble, Cassie Potler, Christina Madsen, Corinne Sullivan, Dani Wong, Danielle Jackson, Darci Miller, Devin MacDonald, Divya Bahl, Elana Altman, Elizabeth Tompkins, Elyssa Goodman, Emily Grier, Erica Avesian, Gabriela Szewcow, Gabriella Cirelli, Gabrielle Sorto, Gennifer Delman, Hannah Orenstein, Heather Rinder, Irene Berman-Vaporis, Iris Goldsztajn, Jamie Blynn, Jaya Z. Powell, Jen Morgan, Jenni Whalen, Jessica Stringer, J'na Jefferson, Judith Ohikuare, Julia Angley, Katie Naymon, Katie Szymanski, Kelsey Damassa, Kelsey Mulvey, Kelsey Pomeroy, Kema Christian-Taylor, Kimya Kavehkar, Laura Hoxworth, Lauren Biscaldi, Lauren Chen, Lauren Kaplan, Lauren Mobertz, Lauren Paylor, Lily Herman, Lola Kolade, Maddie Schmitz, Madeline Harrington, Maggie Walsh, Mariel Loveland, Mary Beth Hills, Maya Devereaux, Meagan Templeton-Lynch, Megan McCluskey, Megan Shuffleton, Meghan DeMaria, Meghan Frick, Michelle King, Nan Zhu, Nancy Mucciarone, Ngozi Ekeledo, Nicole Knoebel, Patricia Ball, Rachel Dozier, Rachel Kossman,

Rebecca Buddingh, Roxanna Coldiron, Sammie Levin, Sara Heath, Sarah Casimong, Sarah Desiderio, Sarah Kahwash, Sophie Dodd, Susannah Hine, Sydney Nolan, Tarina Quraishi, Taylor Trudon, Valentina Palladino, Victoria Uwumarogie, Winnie Ma, and Zoë Renauer.

Lastly, we would like to dedicate this book to our absolutely amazing superstar Her Campus team members all throughout the world, who inspire us every day with their passion for Her Campus's mission and remind us of why we started this company in the first place. Here's to you, collegiettes!

HCXO,

Stephanie, Annie, and Windsor, cofounders of Her Campus

CONTENTS

PART 5: MANAGING YOUR MONEY AND CAREER 269

CHAPTER 18: Managing Your Money 270

CHAPTER 19: Landing Jobs and Internships 281

INTRODUCTION
Hey, Collegiette!

What's a collegiette, you ask? That's you—or, if you're just graduating high school, it will be you in a few short months! *Collegiette* is a term we like to use for a college woman who is on top of her game—strategically career-minded, distinctly fashionable, socially connected, academically driven, and smartly health-conscious—and who endeavors to get the most out of her college experience on every level. Which is pretty much why you're reading this book, right?

So whether you're getting ready to go off to college next fall or are already a seasoned upperclassman (look at you!), you'll find this book chock-full of insider tips and info. First, we'll give you the lowdown on campus safety so you can enjoy all that college has to offer while avoiding the unfortunate scary parts that sometimes come with it. You'll learn how to navigate some of the most important relationships you'll build in college: the ones with your roommates, your professors, and your love interests (ooh la la!). You'll also learn how to handle a relationship when it goes sour, be it with a frenemy or a bad-for-you guy. You'll find every imaginable tip on staying healthy in college, from a fitness and nutrition standpoint as well as when it comes to your physical, mental, and sexual health. We'll tell you how to maximize life *outside* the classroom, through extracurriculars, Greek life, and more, while keeping all of your many pursuits in balance. Plus, we'll take you beyond campus with everything you need to know about managing your money, studying abroad, and scoring jobs and internships to help you transition seamlessly into post-collegiette life (don't worry, you still have time!).

Sprinkled throughout the book you'll also find all sorts of useful resources to help you make our tips a reality, including a sample roommate contract and a dorm-room grocery list.

We hope you enjoy reading *The Her Campus Guide to College Life* as much as we enjoyed putting it together.

Happy reading, collegiettes!

HCXO,

Stephanie, Annie, and Windsor, cofounders of Her Campus

P.S. Want even more from HC? Be sure to check us out online at HerCampus.com and on social media!

PART 1

Staying Safe in College

When you think about preparing for college, you think about textbooks, class schedules, parties, and being away from home. You probably don't think about the dangers of walking around on what looks like an idyllic campus. It probably never crosses your mind that the cute upperclassman in your Psychology 101 class could be a threat. In your excitement about stocking up on fun new items for your dorm and new college life, it doesn't occur to you how susceptible everything is to theft. This isn't to say that your college is some breeding ground for criminal behavior; it's just not the perfect bubble you may have imagined. Bad things happen everywhere, even at college, so you need to be aware! Just as you prepare for life on campus by getting new twin XL sheets, you have to prepare for your safety as well. In the chapters ahead, you'll become prepared for worst-case scenarios: theft, fires, sexual assault, and other things that we hope you never, ever encounter.

CHAPTER 1

Dorm Safety

For the first time ever, you're away from your parents and you're living on your own. You have your own corner in your own dorm room and you've decorated it to be your own college oasis. While your university takes the necessary precautions to keep you safe in your home away from home, there's only so much that fire drills, ID cards, and security can do. And without your parents, the responsibility to keep you and your new home safe is on your shoulders. While hopefully you won't face any threats to your safety in your dorm room, you need to be prepared for the worst-case scenarios—theft, fires, intruders—and do everything in your power to prevent and avoid them.

PREVENTING THEFT

In your first days on campus, everyone seems like a potential BFF. You feel like you're all in it together. You bond quickly with your new friends, and you find yourself trusting them even faster than you thought possible. Unfortunately, not everyone is necessarily as trustworthy as you may think.

What Is at Risk?

Some of the most-stolen items on college campuses are the most valuable things college students own:

- Laptops
- Tablets
- Smartphones
- Jewelry
- Clothing

Your shiny new technology in particular is valuable and easy to swipe, so keeping it safe is definitely important. No one wants to call her parents and tell them she needs money to buy a new laptop, and many professors have little to no patience for the "stolen laptop" excuse if you don't turn in an assignment. Always back your files up every week just in case—use an external hard drive, e-mail drafts of your papers and notes to yourself at a web mail account, or save all of your files to Dropbox. You should always be prepared for the worst-case scenario.

How to Protect Your Technology

At the first level of protection, use a password on your computer—and make it more complex than your last name! Password-protecting your laptop will, at the very least, show your roommate (who will see you log in and out of there countless times) that you're protective of your laptop. It'll also keep nosy roommates from going through your e-mails and Facebook messages, which is especially necessary if you don't get along with them (for more on that, check out Chapter 10).

Advanced Digital Protection for Your Technology

No matter what kind of technology you have, there are ways to protect your property remotely. If you're using an Apple product, set up your iCloud so that your documents are backed up. Equally important is setting up Find My iPhone on all your Apple devices. Having this app will help you track down any iOS device by using any other iOS device, such as your roommate's iPhone.

The powerful app can do more than just locate your device; it can also remotely lock your device, have your device make a sound so you can find it, erase all information on your phone, or display a message on your phone so that in the event it is lost, the finder can return it to you.

Digitally protecting your property is important, but physically protecting your property can be even more important. Thieves, whether they are in your dorm room or in the library, will be immediately deterred once they realize swiping your device won't be easy. Carrying your phone around is no problem when running to the bathroom or to grab a coffee, but your laptop isn't as easy to grab and go with if you need a coffee break while in the library. You can purchase a physical lock at any store that sells laptops. Like a bike lock, you connect the lock to a lock slot (many laptops come equipped with them) and wrap it around a large, bulky object, like a stationary lamp at the library or a desk in your room, so that it's all locked up.

Carrying the lock around may be a pain, but the relief of being able to run outside of the library to answer a call from your BFF 500 miles away without having to first grab your laptop will make it so very worth it.

How to Protect Your Clothes and Jewelry

Jewelry is also stolen often on college campuses. That diamond necklace your grandmother gave you for graduation is easy to swipe from your dresser and even easier for a money-hungry student to pawn. People will constantly be in and out of your room in college—friends, project partners, hook-ups, and complete strangers visiting your roommate. Protect your most valuable objects by investing in a lockbox you keep under your bed, or at the very least, keep your valuables out of sight. As soon as you take off a piece of jewelry, put it somewhere safe. Leaving it out on your dresser or desk is just asking for it to get snatched.

If you're lucky enough to live in a suite-style dorm, always lock your bedroom door, even when your roommates are home. Your suitemates may think you're a bit OCD about locking up, but you'll be grateful when your valuables stay safe! This is especially necessary when you or your roommate is having a big group over for a party or pregame. Be prepared and lock up.

Another huge source of clothing theft is letting friends borrow your clothes. When you go to college, your wardrobe suddenly majorly expands. You need an outfit for a theme party? You have tons of girls you can ask! And they will definitely ask you, too. But especially in the beginning of school, you may find yourself loaning going-out tops and heels to girls you've only known for a short time. And too often, tracking down what you let people borrow becomes a struggle. Or you can't even remember who borrowed what when you finally remember how desperately you need those blue heels back!

While most clothing theft can be chalked up to carelessness on the part of the borrower, there are plenty of girls who think, "I always needed a black top; I'll just 'forget' to return this." In fact, this is probably the most common cause of theft on campus, because it's seemingly so innocuous.

Make it your priority not to forget whom you loaned that top to in the first place by making a note of who borrowed what. It may make you seem a little too organized, but the first friend of yours who can't remember which hallmate borrowed her dress and then can't get it back will be envious of your records. Plus, knowing that you're keeping track of who takes what will keep greedy girls from thinking they can get away with "not returning" your things.

Lastly, laundry theft is a huge issue on college campuses. If your college doesn't offer an app that will tell you when your laundry is done, your safest bet is to sit and wait with your laundry. It's the only way you can avoid people throwing your clothes on the floor (which is just plain rude!) or swiping something of yours.

Locking Up

But truly, the most important way to prevent theft (and unasked borrowing) is locking your door every single time you leave. You may think you're just going to the bathroom for a second and it's fine, but then you peek into your friend's room and start chatting with her, all while your door remains unlocked and your belongings are left at risk.

FIRE SAFETY

According to the National Fire Protection Association, there are between 3,350 and 4,220 fires every year in the dormitory occupancy group. Not surprisingly, cooking is overwhelmingly responsible for these fires. Think about it: When you used to cook at home, your mom or dad was always there reminding you to turn down the stove, not to put metal in the microwave, and to turn off the oven when you're done. In college, there's no one breathing down your neck reminding you to be careful, so it's all on you.

Preventing Fires

When cooking, the number-one thing you can do to prevent a fire from breaking out in your dorm (and to prevent making enemies of your dormmates) is to monitor your cooking. Leaving your food on the stove and running out to let a friend into your building or to watch the rest of your favorite TV show in the common room is an easy way for something to catch on fire and for you not to notice until it's too late. So plan your cooking time well: If you know something is going to distract you, wait to put your food on heat.

Another major source of fires is items catching on fire near the cooking area. Again, your parents at home know not to keep paperwork near the stove, but on your first cooking adventures, you may find yourself studying for your Bio 101 midterm as you make tacos. Having those biology notes catch on fire would mean more tragedy than just lost notes (which is definitely a tragedy). So keep things that can easily catch on fire, like papers, dishtowels, and loose-fitting sleeves, away from flames.

Be prepared by locating where the nearest fire extinguisher is before you start cooking. A lot of small fires can be easily extinguished, but it is important to know how to use the fire extinguisher—and where it is! You've seen them around your whole life, but odds are you've never used one or even seen it in use.

What to Do in the Event of a Small Fire

There is a pin at the top of the extinguisher that you will pull out that effectively unlocks the extinguisher. Once it's unlocked, aim the extinguisher at the base of the fire (where it started) and slowly squeeze the lever to release the extinguishing agent. Sweep the extinguisher back and forth so the chemical can cover all aspects of the fire.

However, do *not* plan on taking everything into your own hands. Still call, or have someone else call, 911 so that if a small fire cannot be contained, the fire department will already be on their way over.

Other Sources of Fire

As you can imagine, most colleges do everything they can to prevent fires by limiting which items are allowed in dorm rooms. Most colleges forbid candles (yes, even birthday candles!), hookahs, smoking, and incense in the rooms for this very reason. But college students often aren't the best rule followers, so these items do get snuck into the dorm rooms anyway (and then those students are often slapped with hefty fines and punishments!).

Make sure your dorm room is free of these potentially dangerous items, but also protect your community by gently reminding your hallmates of these rules. If you see someone lighting a cigarette in his dorm room, you shouldn't hesitate for a second to suggest that he take that outside. If you go visit a friend's room and she's lighting incense or candles, remind of her of the rules and consequences. For birthdays, suggest having cake outdoors or at a restaurant.

If for some reason people seem completely unaffected by your gentle reminders, there's nothing wrong with providing your RA (resident assistant) with an anonymous tip that someone is breaking serious rules. Better safe than sorry!

PROTECTING AGAINST INTRUDERS

Many colleges, especially those in large cities, have security guards in dorm lobbies who check IDs and have all residents check their visitors into the dorms. But more suburban and rural schools often lack these checkpoints and simply require a swipe of your ID card or fob to enter the building.

In the beginning of the school year, it's almost inevitable that you'll forget your fob or that your ID card will become demagnetized and you won't be able to get into your building. Kind neighbors will open the door for you and let you follow them in. Is this nice? Of course. Is it also dangerous? Definitely.

While you think you can probably deduce who is a college student and who doesn't belong in your dorm, it's not exactly a foolproof plan. It's scary to think about, but if you were a cute, eighteen-year-old thief, don't you think you might try to sneak into dorms and steal things? You'd certainly have no issue getting into the building with all those "nice" people letting you in.

Your RA will definitely warn you of all these risks in your first hall and dorm meetings, but many people feel guilty not letting those who look like they belong into the building. They think, "I don't want to be the jerk who doesn't let that girl in who is stuck without a key in the rain." However, you *really* don't want to be the jerk that lets in a hostile intruder.

What to Ask to Determine If Someone Is a Student Before Letting Her Into Your Dorm

You don't want to be the crazy person interrogating your hall-mates with a million questions just so they can get into the building, but there are friendly, innocuous ways of determining whether or not the person asking to be let into your building is a criminal or just a college student. Odds are you'll have at least a few seconds to walk with him or her, so here are some innocent questions you can ask that will just make you seem curious, and not like a self-assigned campus police officer. We recommend that you don't ask *all* of the questions (unless it's become a normal, back-and-forth, well-flowing conversation).

- I don't think we've met. What's your name?
- What floor do you live on?
- Oh, the fourth floor? I'm always up there visiting Katie Smith; do you live near her?
- Do you have a roommate? What's her name?
- What's your suite number?
- What's your major?

The best way to balance being the jerk that didn't let an actual resident in and the jerk who let an intruder in is to consistently not let people follow you in by avoiding the situation to begin with. If someone suspicious-looking is lingering around the front door of your dorm, maybe this isn't such a good time to head inside that way. Someone with malicious intent probably isn't going to wait very long to get into your building, since that will just make the person look even more suspicious! Even if the person looks completely innocent, you may want to delay going inside until the person has moved on or someone who's obviously a friend of the loiterer has let him or her in so that you aren't letting non-residents into your building.

If someone does end up getting into your building, either via you or via another hallmate, don't be afraid to head in that person's direction to see where he or she is going. Hey, it's your dorm; you can walk around wherever you want! If the person is lingering and seeming lost without a convincing explanation, never hesitate to call campus security (a number you should definitely have programmed into your phone!).

Wellness Check-In: Pack These Five Things for Dorm Safety

1. **Lockbox:** Store your most valuable possessions in a lockbox to prevent theft by everyone from friends and roommates to professional thieves. This will keep your jewelry and valuable trinkets safe.
2. **Laptop lock:** Invest in a laptop lock that will anchor your computer to a bulky item, such as your desk. This will keep less determined thieves from moving your things around and leave you less vulnerable to theft.
3. **Keychain:** Put your keys on something easy to locate in your backpack so that you don't lose them. This is your first line of defense against thieves.
4. **Pepper spray:** Odds are that you'll never use it, but it won't hurt to have a small pepper spray in your purse,

in your backpack, or even on your keychain in the event that you feel threatened when traveling through campus. Just make sure it's legal to carry in the state where you go to school.

5. **Campus Safety phone numbers:** Before you even get on campus, find the numbers for campus safety and any other services for walking students home at night or helping students in danger. Store these in your cell phone—you never know when you'll need them, and you don't want to waste time searching for them when you do!

Chapter Checklist

✓ Protect your technology with passwords, location apps, and physical locks.

✓ Protect your jewelry by using a lockbox and storing it in an out-of-sight place, such as under your bed.

✓ Keep track of who borrows what from you to prevent accidental theft.

✓ Monitor your laundry when washing clothes to prevent clothing theft.

✓ Always watch any cooked food you prepare to avoid kitchen fires.

✓ Keep flammable objects, such as class notes, away from open flames when cooking.

✓ Be aware of how to properly use a fire extinguisher.

✓ Don't let strangers in your dorm.

✓ Don't hesitate to call campus safety or alert an RA if there is anyone suspicious-looking lurking around your dorm.

✓ Lock your door!

CHAPTER 2

Safety Around Campus

Your first day on your college campus will feel so full of promise—this is the place you'll start to really map out your future as an adult, meet lifelong friends, and make many meaningful memories. However, in order to keep your memories positive, you need to stay safe on campus. This is a different world than the one you're used to back home, and it comes with its own unique set of safety concerns and tools for staying safe.

STAYING SAFE AT PARTIES AND BARS

College parties should be fun, and they (almost always) are. But there are also a number of safety concerns when partying with a bunch of strangers.

Keeping Your Drink Safe

When you go to a party, expect to have someone offer to get you a drink or make you a drink, but be wary of accepting a drink you didn't see get prepared. If you choose to drink, be safe about it: Don't put your drink down and come back later and drink from it, don't take a drink from the mysterious punch bowl, and don't let anyone else get your drink for you. The only way you will know exactly what you're drinking is if you watch where it comes from and never leave your glass unattended. Your best bet is to drink a can of beer that you open yourself.

We can't stress enough how important it is to watch your drink—don't set it down or even let that cute guy hang on to it while you go to the bathroom, no matter how much you think you can trust him. There is no foolproof way of telling if that guy is actually a nice guy or if he's planning on slipping something dangerous, like a date rape drug, into your cup. And don't get so drunk that you'll have a hard time keeping track of where you put your drink.

There are also plenty of personal safety concerns you should be aware of before you decide to drink. Check out Chapter 7 for more information on drinking in college.

Know What They're Talking About: Code Names for Rohypnol (the "Date Rape" Drug)

This list provided by WomensHealth.gov: Rophies (pronounced ROOF-eez); Roofies; Ruffies; Forget-me pill; Mexican Valium; Roaches; Rope; Roples; Wolfies; Circles; Reynolds.

This is just a small list of nicknames for this dangerous drug, which is a central nervous system depressant. But it should give you an idea of what to listen for when you hear guys acting sneaky and aggressive about making you or a friend an unknown drink or taking your drink from you.

Medical Amnesty

College parties should be fun! You should be dancing, meeting people, and letting loose after a long week of papers, tests, and lectures. But too often people let *too* loose and end up drinking way more than they should. You should never hesitate to seek medical attention for someone who seems too drunk (e.g., cannot walk, is throwing up, is incredibly disoriented).

Many students worry that if they seek medical attention for themselves or their friends who are drinking underage, they'll get in trouble. Fortunately, many schools offer medical amnesty in these situations.

Medical amnesty initiatives, also known as Good Samaritan or 911 protection laws, are essentially policies that are put in place to protect you and your friends from facing harsh legal consequences in a drug- or alcohol-related emergency. In almost all instances, medical amnesty initiatives will only cover you in terms of protection from legal consequences related to drinking or doing drugs. That is, if you're involved in something else illegal at the time you call for help—such as property damage, theft, or assault—the amnesty policy usually won't protect you from anything except legal charges related to underage drinking or drugs.

It's also important to note that most local medical amnesty policies shield you from harsh legal consequences, such as possession charges or even an overnight jail trip, but don't protect you from university-sponsored punishments or disciplinary action. Most students who call for help under the protection of medical amnesty can still face university-mandated consequences, possibly including community service, alcohol education classes through the college health center, or parental notification. However, policies vary from school to school, so it's a good idea to become familiar with your college or university's written policy regarding medical amnesty. Overall, keep in mind that if you fear you or a friend is dangerously ill from drinking, immediately getting the necessary medical attention is always more important than what consequences you might suffer.

Stick with Friends

You should never, ever go to a party alone. You would probably feel awkward in a huge party, sitting all by your lonesome, anyway. Going to a party alone is unsafe.

But, just as importantly, you also shouldn't ditch your friends (or let them ditch you—what kind of girlfriends are those?!) once you walk in the door to go hang out with some guy. The last thing you want is to be alone when that creepy senior offers you a mystery drink he got from a closed room.

Having a buddy is great because she'll wait in inevitably long bathroom lines with you, she can rescue you from an aggressive guy on the dance floor, and she'll also walk or cab back to the dorms with you.

Make Smart Decisions about Fake IDs

You usually start college at age eighteen, and it isn't legal to drink until you turn twenty-one, so some students get fake IDs in the hopes of getting into college town bars and buying alcohol at liquor stores.

Aside from the fact that it's illegal, getting a fake ID and using it comes with a plethora of risks. Getting a fake ID can be super tempting when you can't get into the bars and clubs your older friends are buzzing about, but it's essential for collegiettes to be aware of the potential penalties of using a fake ID before you flash one to a bouncer.

Most bouncers in college areas are extra careful when they check IDs, making sure your eye color matches what it says on your ID, seeing if you know your area code, and often asking for backup identification, such as a credit card. If the bouncer determines it's a fake ID, he may just reject you, or he may reject you and have you give him your fake ID, or he may report you to the establishment, which might then pursue legal action.

The penalties for having a fake ID, using one, manufacturing one, or impersonating a person on an ID that isn't yours vary depending on the state. It's important to go to your state's Alcohol and Beverage Commission website to get the official laws.

The consequences for producers of fake IDs are hefty. For example, in the state of Missouri, the forgery of a government-issued identity document is a felony. It is punishable by up to seven years in prison and/or a fine up to $5,000. No one wants to explain that one to her parents. So definitely consider these potential consequences before getting a fake!

BEING SAFE WHILE HOOKING UP

If you decide to "hang out" at a guy's place after a party, let your friends know who the guy is (and make sure you are coherent enough to know who this guy is yourself!), where he lives, and when you expect to be home. Always have cash with you in case you need to get out immediately and take a cab home.

You should always plan on having an exit strategy when heading off with a guy so that in the event that he makes you uncomfortable (or you're just ready to go back to your own bed), you can get home without relying on him.

Exit Strategy

1. Fully charge your cell phone before going out. The last thing you want is a dead cell phone when trying to leave some guy's apartment (or heading there to begin with!).

2. Pre-program local cab numbers and/or ridesharing apps on your phone so you can easily get a ride back to your dorm.

3. Know where you are! Ask him on the way to his place where you're headed so you know how far you are from your dorm and can mentally prepare in the event that you decide to leave early.

4. Don't worry about offending him if you decide to leave. Your reason for leaving is your business, and you shouldn't let him influence it.

5. Of course, if you decide to stay the night, be safe about your hook-ups! Don't let anyone pressure you to do anything more

than you're comfortable with (more about that in later chapters), and be prepared for safe sex. Most non–religiously affiliated schools offer free condoms at on-campus health centers. Don't ever let someone pressure you into unprotected sex, no matter what.

STAYING SAFE LATE AT NIGHT

While walking around campus from class to class during the day is generally safe, nighttime presents unique challenges to your safety. The best way you can keep yourself safe on campus is by utilizing the buddy system. You are far less attractive to stalkers, muggers, and other malicious people when you're not alone. If you study late at night at the library, bring a friend who's on a similar work schedule so she can walk back with you. And again, if you're partying, definitely be with at least one friend, since you're more at risk after you've been drinking.

No Friends to Walk Back With?
Four Ways of Getting Back Safely

Blue Lights: Many campuses provide Blue Lights, which are security systems in fixed locations on campus. When you make a call from a Blue Light, campus police officers are notified and they will escort you home or help you deal with an issue, such as a suspicious person nearby.

Escorts: Many schools offer a transportation system or volunteer escorts who will safely help you around school. Ask your RA if your school offers this.

Activate "Find My Friends": Activate this app on your phone so that if something were to happen to you, your friends would be able to more easily find you.

Call the Police: Get a number for non-emergencies for the local police department and save it in your phone before you get to campus.

Protecting Yourself When You Are Alone

If you do end up walking by yourself, don't stop moving. Spend as little time as possible lingering outside your residence. As you approach your building, start to take out your keys so you can head right in. Don't stop in the middle of the sidewalk or in front of your building because you need to answer a friend's text.

You can also call a friend or family member to talk to on the phone as you walk home. But be careful; don't get so wrapped up in a conversation that you don't realize someone might be following you. You want to stay as aware as possible when moving around campus and the surrounding areas at night. On the same note, be careful of wearing headphones with the music turned up loud while walking alone, as this will make you less likely to hear or notice anything going on nearby that you should be aware of.

If you find yourself habitually walking around campus at night, seriously consider carrying pepper spray in your purse or backpack if it's legal in your school's state. This will give you confidence when traipsing across campus in the evening, will provide an immediate line of defense against a person with malicious intent, and could potentially save your life.

STALKERS

You may kid around with your friends about "Facebook stalking" crushes or exes, but trust us: Real stalkers are no joke. Whether your stalker is an ex-boyfriend who just won't move on or, more unlikely, someone you don't know, his or her behavior must be taken seriously.

In the event that you do have a stalker, first you must record everything he or she is doing. Print threatening e-mails, take screenshots of and save menacing text messages, and record when you feel violated by noting it in a journal or someplace on your computer, with the date, time, and what occurred. Literally having a file on your stalker before you end up having to seek legal action will give you a much stronger case, if it does come to that.

Warn your friends about your stalker. Don't keep your fears to yourself. Show friends who might not know your stalker what the person looks like. Pull photos from Facebook to show them (and save them for your file!).

Don't overshare. If you have a stalker, it is a terrible idea to post things on Facebook like "Studying late at the library! Come visit me!" Unless you want your stalker to bring you a coffee and follow you through the library stacks, we suggest keeping your location to yourself and those you trust, not sharing it with just anyone with access to your social media pages.

Finally, if you have a stalker, be smart and never explore campus alone, especially at night. Utilize friends, Blue Lights, and campus escorts and consider involving the police, who can help you pursue a restraining order.

PREVENTING CAR BREAK-INS

Having a car at college can make your life easier in some ways, but can also be a major pain in others. Not only have you become the go-to girl for grocery store runs, trips to the mall, and airport/bus drop-offs, but also for the first time you're solely responsible for keeping your car safe.

With few schools offering parking garages, your car is probably going to be sitting in a lot most of the time, at risk of theft. And we really mean most of the time: You definitely won't drive your car as much as you think you will at college. You'll mostly be walking around.

To keep your car and the things you store in it safe, consider the following:

Lock Your Car

Always. Maybe you didn't have to lock your car when it sat in your parents' driveway every day, but college is a different situation.

So always lock your car and, no matter the heat, roll up your windows. Don't make it easy for thieves!

Conceal Valuables

If you leave your laptop on your passenger seat, viewable to anyone who walks by, you're asking for trouble. If you insist on keeping valuables in the car, cover them up or store them in the trunk. This means shopping bags, iPods, GPS systems, and anything else you wouldn't want stolen!

But Don't Let People See You Storing Valuable Items in the Trunk, Either

If there is a suspicious-looking person lurking around the parking lot, don't let him or her watch as you move valuable things to your trunk. You might as well scream, "I'm putting expensive things in the trunk! That's where all the good stuff is!" If there's no way to discreetly hide your valuables in your car, keep the items on you if possible rather than leaving them exposed in the car.

Park in a Well-Lit Area

If space is available, always park as close as you can to campus buildings and street lamps. This is a small line of defense that could make a big difference when someone is deciding which car to break into.

Purchase Key Items to Protect Your Car

Particularly if your school isn't located in the safest of places, consider adding the following to your shopping list to increase the safety of your car.

Car Alarm

Even if your car didn't come with an alarm, you can still purchase one. While alarms that come installed in your car tend to be best, any alarm is usually better than no alarm.

Steering Wheel Lock

This is an affordable, highly visible theft deterrent. It is a metal bar that is locked to your steering wheel and makes moving your car impossible.

Brake Pedal Lock

Another highly visible theft deterrent, the brake pedal lock works by preventing the brake or clutch pedal from being depressed, which makes driving impossible. Like steering wheel locks, these are also very affordable.

Wellness Check-In: Three Rules to Make with Your Friends Before Leaving Any Party

Stick Together!

It's unrealistic to think you and the five girls you came to the party with are never going to separate, but plan on sticking with one friend throughout the night. It's best if this is a friend with similar party interests as you (e.g., you two have like-minded opinions about drinking and drugs, what time you like to go home, and late-night, post-party hook-ups).

Watch Each Other's Back

If your friend looks away from her drink, make sure no one slips anything in it when she's not paying attention. If a friend is being aggressively pursued on the dance floor, be prepared to rescue her from the guy. And talk soberly beforehand about how to handle a drunk friend—especially if you have that belligerent friend who does not like to be told she's had enough.

Safely Separate

If you or your friend heads off to be alone with a guy, make sure you do the following before leaving.

- Introduce your friend to the guy. This way they know each other, and your friend knows whom you're going off with.
- Make sure you have a fully charged phone so you can stay in touch with friends and get home easily if you feel uncomfortable.
- Let your friend know where you ended up and when you get back to your dorm so she knows you're safe.

Chapter Checklist

- ✓ If you choose to drink at parties, don't drink from mysterious punch bowls! Either watch someone make your drink or open a can of beer yourself (the safest option!).
- ✓ Don't abandon your drink or let anyone slip anything into your cup.
- ✓ If your friend is sick from alcohol, do not be afraid to seek medical attention for her. Most schools offer medical amnesty, so the legal consequences for underage drinking will be lessened or eliminated.
- ✓ Stay with your friends! Go to parties with a group, but pick one friend to stick with the whole night.

✓ Weigh the pros and cons of a fake ID before getting one. The consequences can be incredibly detrimental to your bright future!

✓ Be safe while hooking up by keeping your friends looped in about your location and having a fully charged phone so you can get out of uncomfortable situations.

✓ Don't be afraid to ask someone to walk home with you, whether it's a friend, classmate, dormmate, escort, or even the police! Better safe than sorry!

✓ Concerned you have a stalker? Document every threat you receive, don't publicize your location, and never hesitate to call the police.

✓ Lock your car and hide valuables to prevent car break-ins.

✓ Park in well-lit, busy areas to prevent attacks and theft.

CHAPTER 3

Sexual Assault

Trigger warning: This chapter contains information about sexual assault and violence, which may be triggering to survivors.

In a study of undergraduate women, the Centers for Disease Control and Prevention found that 19 percent of collegiettes experienced attempted or completed sexual assault since entering college. That's nearly one in five collegiettes.

Unfortunately, odds are that even if you never experience this kind of traumatic violence, someone you know will. With that in mind, it's important to know how to protect yourself, report assailants, help your friends who are victims of sexual violence, and get the help you need if you become a victim of sexual assault.

UNDERSTANDING AND PREVENTING SEXUAL ASSAULT

In a report compiled by the New York State Coalition Against Sexual Assault, almost 50 percent of those who experienced unwanted sexual activity did not consider the case to be assault. Before you can properly protect yourself—especially from those you know and think you can trust—you should know how to define sexual assault so that you're fully aware when you are a victim.

The U.S. Department of Justice defines sexual assault as "any type of sexual contact or behavior that occurs without the explicit consent of the recipient. Falling under the definition of sexual assault are sexual activities such as forced sexual intercourse, forcible sodomy, child molestation, incest, fondling, and attempted rape."

Consent and Sexual Assault

Any time both people cannot give consent, it is considered sexual assault. When you're intoxicated, you cannot give consent. The absence of saying "no" is not consent; consent is signified by a clear, unambiguous "yes," whether that's verbal or conveyed otherwise. Being in a relationship with someone does not qualify as consent. Any time you decline consent and it is violated—no matter if it's violated by a stranger, friend, or boyfriend, and no matter what you've done (or worn) leading up to the moment of consent—it is sexual assault.

Acquaintance Rape

According to the Rape, Abuse & Incest National Network (RAINN), "acquaintance assault involves coercive sexual activities that occur against a person's will by means of force, violence, duress, or fear of bodily injury. These sexual activities are imposed upon them by someone they know (a friend, date, acquaintance, etc.)." This could be a friend, classmate, partner, or ex-partner. In the report compiled by the New York State Coalition Against Sexual Assault, 80 percent of rape victims were assaulted by an acquaintance.

Acquaintance rape is even more common on college campuses than in the general population. One reason acquaintance rape happens so frequently on college campuses is because of the congested atmosphere of young adults all living together. A lot of sexual crime already occurs with people in this age bracket, but living together increases the frequency of these crimes to an even greater extent.

Plus, you might often feel that if you're in a class with someone, you know that person. This can lead you to trust someone even though you really don't know him or her very well. Or, even if you really do know the person, that unfortunately still doesn't mean that he or she isn't capable of sexual violence.

Acquaintance rape can emotionally harm the victim by causing the victim to struggle with his or her ability to trust others. Often, the assailant is someone the victim thought he or she could trust. Because that trust was taken away, this makes the victim question who he or she can possibly trust, if anyone. A sexual assault victim should never be afraid to seek help from a therapist, especially after an incident of this type.

Protecting Yourself

There are a number of ways you can reduce your risk of sexual assault.

Consider this: In the report compiled by the New York State Coalition Against Sexual Assault, 50 percent of sexual assault cases were reported to have occurred when either the victims or the perpetrators were under the influence of alcohol, and almost 60 percent of cases occurred when individuals were on a date.

Completely avoiding going on dates and/or (for many people) drinking certainly aren't the solutions here (both can be very fun when done responsibly!), but being vigilant when drinking and when dating can be a solution.

By exercising responsible behaviors, you should be able to go out and drink with your friends or go on a date without living in fear of sexual assault.

To lessen your risk while drinking:

Drink in Moderation

Drinking not only impairs your judgment, but also removes your ability to consent.

Stick with Friends While Drinking

Being with friends means you won't be alone. Also, consider a code word or signal with your friends that signifies when you are feeling uncomfortable and need someone to help you out of the situation.

Keep an Eye on Your Drink

If you lose sight of your drink for a moment, get a new one. Better to waste a drink than to potentially end up with a date rape drug in your system.

Charge Your Phone

Always have a fully charged cell phone so you can communicate with your friends and escape a potentially dangerous situation if need be.

Trust Your Instincts

If that guy you're debating going home with seems a little sketchy, suggest meeting up for coffee the next day instead and nix the late-night hook-up.

Date in Public Places

It's not a date if you're just watching a movie back in his dorm room (a definite place for a greater risk of acquaintance rape); it's a hook-up. For a real and safe date, go to a busy restaurant. Be around other people. There is nothing wrong with taking it slow and avoiding being alone together before you feel you can trust someone.

Set Limits

Whether you verbalize them or not, mentally prepare yourself for what you would be comfortable doing on a date. Then, follow through with your pre-determined limits.

Don't Assume You Can Trust Someone

You shouldn't live your life in fear of strangers, but you should always exercise caution. In high school, you probably knew most of the guys your whole life. You knew their parents, their younger siblings, and where they live. In college, odds are you know next to nothing about the guys. Just because someone has a peripheral connection to someone you know (e.g., he's your new BFF's lab partner) does not mean you should immediately put all your trust in him. Trust must be earned in relationships.

While being cautious may lessen the risk of an attack, it cannot always prevent rape from occurring.

While an assault or rape can be devastating, it is important to remember that even if you took all possible precautions, such things can still happen—and they are still not your fault. Sexual assault is *never* your fault.

REPORTING SEXUAL ASSAULT

Many psychologists refer to sexual assault as "the silent epidemic" because many people who have been sexually assaulted don't report the incident. But why is that?

Part of the reason behind this ties back to the definition of sexual assault. When someone mentions "sexual assault," the images of a violent attacker, weapons, and a dark alley come to mind. However, as mentioned before, sexual assault is actually defined as "any type of sexual contact or behavior that occurs without the explicit consent of the recipient." Sexual assault is often unreported because many collegiettes don't identify an unwanted sexual experience as sexual assault.

Another piece of this silent epidemic puzzle is the fact that sexual assault often occurs with someone you know. Whether it is a consistent hook-up, a former boyfriend, or a one-night stand, many cases of sexual assault (especially in college) are acquaintance rapes. It is much easier to feel hatred and want to press charges against someone who attacked you in a dark alley; it is much more difficult to go to the authorities to report someone you had a crush on, but just didn't want to go that far with.

However, by not reporting your assault, you are perpetuating the crime. By not reporting the crime, you are leaving others at risk of feeling the same way you do and being in the same position you were in and are in, at the hands of the same person.

If you do choose to report your sexual abuse, you can either report it directly to the police or go to the hospital for a rape kit or other medical attention, and they will call the police for you. While you can report your rape months after it occurred, the sooner you report, the better, so that DNA samples can be collected. But you may not want to relive the incident right away, which is understandable.

If the victim is unsure if protection was used, it's important to have a medical exam to check for pregnancy or sexually transmitted infections (STIs), whether or not it is part of a larger forensic medical exam.

Unfortunately, whether you choose to press charges or report the incident or not, the consequences of the attack continue psychologically. Seeking help for the emotional aftermath of the assault can be just as important as seeking help for the initial physical trauma.

While everyone responds very differently to a traumatic event like this, one of the most common initial responses is blaming oneself. But again, sexual assault is never the victim's fault, even if he or she had been drinking beforehand.

The Rape Kit

It is your decision, and only your decision, to go to the hospital for a forensic examination following sexual assault. According to RAINN, during the exam, a rape kit (or sexual assault evidence collection kit) may be used. This kit is used to collect any DNA that may have been left by the suspect.

The exam, which is typically a full body examination, may include collection of blood, urine, hair, and other body secretion samples. Photos of your body may be taken, as well as collection of undergarments and any other relevant clothing, and any physical evidence taken from the scene of the crime.

There is a whole range of reactions that victims have after a rape occurs. Some people don't tell anyone about the incident because they find it easier to cope by keeping their feelings inside. Others need to tell someone, and feel that talking about it helps them move forward. Some people don't eat after the event; others will eat more. Some people will sleep a lot; some won't be able to fall asleep. Some people won't be able to focus on academics; others will focus more on their work.

HELPING YOURSELF OR A FRIEND WHO EXPERIENCED SEXUAL ASSAULT

If you (or a friend) are a victim of sexual assault, you must make decisions that you are comfortable with in terms of seeking help. Here are a few options for sharing the trauma with trusted people, whether or not you report it to the authorities.

Talk to a Professional

Your campus should have some place where you can talk to a counselor about what happened to you. If for some reason this service is not available on campus, you should be able to find a professional to talk to in the surrounding area.

Read about It

If talking about the experience is too upsetting, sometimes just reading a booklet from a counseling center for survivors of sexual abuse can help you to cope.

Turn to a Trusted Friend

Confiding in a friend is a way to digest what happened to you.

Learning Resources

There is a ton of information online to help you cope. You just need to know where to look! Safe Horizon (*www.safehorizon.org*) has a "Recovery Guide for Survivors" on their website that you can download for free. RAINN (*www.rainn.org*) has tons of information on their site about recovery from sexual assault, including how to help a loved one, if this happened to your friend. After Silence (*www.aftersilence.org*) is an online support group for victims of rape, sexual assault, and sexual abuse.

As the victim's friend, you will want to unquestioningly support her. If she confides in you about what happened, make sure you ask if there's anything you can do to help. However, avoid telling her what she should and should not do. Even if you value talking things out to solve problems, your friend may not feel the same way, or vice versa. Equally important is making sure not to judge. You may likely know the perpetrator, but saying things like "Joe is such a nice guy! I can't believe he would do that" isn't helpful, nor is saying, "Oh, come on! You sleep with everyone when you drink; why is Joe any different?"

Also, make sure you don't treat your friend any differently than you did before she confided in you. Victims won't want every conversation to revolve around what happened; usually, they want you to treat them the same as always, but to just be aware that they're going through a difficult time.

However, victims will appreciate you checking in with them every once in a while. After someone confides in you, it's reassuring if you pull that friend aside sometimes and let her know you're thinking of her.

If your friend wants to report the assault, encourage her, accompany her if she would like, and support her. No one should have to go to the police station or hospital alone if they do not want to. But don't be aggressive in your willingness to accompany—be gentle!

Finally, empower your friend! Her power was just taken away by her assailant; she needs you to help her feel safe, in control, supported, and respected by standing by her throughout this ordeal.

Wellness Check-In: Add These Three Contact Numbers to Your Phone Just in Case

In the event of a sexual assault, you may find it too difficult to confide in a friend, seek professional help, or report what happened to the police. But you may want to tell someone who can give you advice, help you cope, and give you the feeling of anonymity. Save the number for the National Sexual Assault Hotline (800-656-HOPE) in your phone. They will connect you with the nearest RAINN member center. Your call is confidential and anonymous. And because they connect you with someone local, the person you speak to will be properly equipped to discuss the rape and sexual assault laws in your state.

Additionally, you should also save the number of your local police department and the number of the nearest hospital in your cell phone, just in case!

Chapter Checklist

✓ Understand that sexual assault is "any type of sexual contact or behavior that occurs without the explicit consent of the recipient."

✓ While you can never completely prevent sexual assault, you can lessen your risk by drinking and dating more safely.

✓ Do not be afraid to report sexual assault.

✓ If you or a friend is the victim, consider speaking to a professional, reading about how to cope and recover from the incident, and talking to trusted friends.

✓ If a friend confides in you after she is assaulted, ask how you can help, assist her in taking any necessary legal or medical steps, do not judge her, and avoid asking too many questions.

CHAPTER 4

Studying Abroad

Picture it: You're in a beautiful new country, surrounded by an entirely new culture and making memories that will last a lifetime. Studying abroad is one of the greatest opportunities available to you in college. Traveling and exploring other cultures is not only fun, but is also a great educational experience. You can use the time to earn school credit, volunteer overseas, explore a new career, or even learn the secrets to Italian cooking!

Of course, making the decision to study abroad is a big one. There are so many things to consider, such as cost, location, staying safe in a new country, and timing. Whether you just started to think about studying abroad or you've had a poster of Greece above your bed since you read *Sisterhood of the Traveling Pants* (we get it—we want to be in Santorini with a Kostas, too!), it's important to cover all of your bases before you hop on that plane.

DECIDING TO STUDY ABROAD

So, you want to study abroad. Great! However, there are still many other factors to consider before you can book your ticket and start adding European weekend trip ideas to your Pinterest travel board. The earlier you ask these questions and do your research, the better.

Major Requirements

Before you even begin the process of exploring programs, it's best to meet with your academic advisor to make sure that you can afford to spend a semester off campus. Depending on your major and your previous coursework, missing a semester might mean missing required courses or credits.

Language Skills, Goals, and Requirements

When making the decision to study abroad, it's crucial that you keep your language goals in mind. Do you want to become fluent in the native tongue of the city, or are you looking to explore a city while working or studying in English? Some programs might have language requirements, while others might allow you to enroll in an international school where classes are taught in English. Researching housing options for any potential programs is also important because living in a homestay will give you more of a chance to practice the language than would living in an apartment with other American students.

Program and Travel Costs

If you normally receive financial aid, there's a chance you'll be able to get assistance abroad, too, but make sure to talk to both your school's study abroad and financial aid offices well in advance of applying. Talk to former participants to see how much money they spent while abroad and if they were able to work while overseas, and make sure you look into tuition, housing, and meal plan costs before you leave.

Creative Ways to Fulfill Academic Requirements Abroad

While the majority of your major requirements will need to be completed at your home institution, keep an eye out for opportunities to fulfill other academic requirements. If your school requires a class on subjects such as art history or cultural diversity, see if you can fulfill those classes abroad and make room for more electives on campus.

Additionally, if you're attending a university where classes are taught in a foreign language, double-check whether they will count for credits toward a foreign language minor. There's nothing quite like learning about Michelangelo while you're looking at the ceiling of the Sistine Chapel!

HOW TO FIND AND CHOOSE A STUDY ABROAD PROGRAM

Once you've determined that you are able to study abroad and know which time of year you'd like to go, the next step is nailing down the location. There are many different factors to take into account, from language and location to type of experience and cost.

Finding a Program

Many different resources and tools are available to students looking to study abroad. The first step is scheduling a meeting with your school's study abroad office to learn more about the internal programs they offer and any external relationships they might have. Many schools also offer study abroad info sessions with panels of students who previously studied abroad so that you can get a student's perspective.

Internal programs are programs run by your college or university. You'll typically be with people from your school, and your college may even have its own special campus set up in other parts of the world. If you want to study in a city or country where you don't speak the language, finding a program where your classes are mostly taught in English might be something to consider.

External programs are programs run by other colleges and universities or by study abroad companies. If your school's internal programs don't travel to locations you're interested in or the timing isn't quite right, external opportunities might be for you. Many study abroad offices have information on external programs, and many schools have partnerships with external programs so that your credits will easily transfer.

Choosing a Program

Narrowing down your program options is a huge accomplishment, but now you're left with a choice: Which program is the perfect program for you?

Every city in the world offers a different cultural experience, and where you choose to study abroad will have a huge effect on the months ahead. As much as your time abroad will be about studying, working, or volunteering, it will be even more about exploring and fitting into a new environment and absorbing the culture around you. So, when considering where to study, you should first ask yourself what kind of feel you want your abroad location to have. Do you want a big, cosmopolitan city where you'll be able to speak English? Consider London. Want a smaller city where you'll be forced to speak Spanish all the time? Maybe Granada is more for you.

It's also important to consider your city of choice's location on a world map. As much as you may be dying to volunteer in Papua New Guinea, it may not be the most convenient place for weekend trips to France and Italy. Choosing a central location will make train and plane tickets cheap and easy for international travel. And don't forget to look up the weather: When it's summer in the States, it's winter in the Southern Hemisphere, and vice versa—so Buenos Aires may be a better choice for a winter or spring semester abroad than for a summer stay.

Whichever program you choose, the important thing is to make sure it's the right program for you. Your friends and classmates will probably be traveling to various different parts of the world, but make sure not to compare those experiences or choices. You'll be so much happier with your decision if you're honest and realistic about what will work best for you!

AFFORDING YOUR TIME ABROAD

If you're studying abroad through your school, first check with your financial aid office to see what fees your regular tuition will cover. Typically your tuition will cover your abroad tuition fees through any internal programs, but housing, travel, and other costs will be extra. Once you've figured out how much it will cost you to study abroad, there are a few different ways of financing any remaining costs.

Talk to a Financial Aid Advisor

Your financial aid advisor is one of the first people you should talk to before jetting off for your semester overseas. If you already receive federal financial aid, such as a Pell Grant, chances are that that aid can be applied to your semester abroad as well. In some cases, your school may even be able to give you extra money to cover the additional costs of studying at a foreign institution. Make sure to add up all of the expenses ahead of time to find out exactly how much your semester abroad will cost you and how much extra funding you may need.

Before making an appointment with an advisor, be sure to come up with a list of good questions to ask, such as:

- How much will it cost to study abroad, including housing and extra expenses?
- Will my financial aid be applicable to my semester abroad?
- Can I extend my financial aid package to cover the extra costs of studying abroad?
- Will I pay my home university's tuition, or the tuition of the foreign institution?

You could also consider taking out a loan to help pay for your tuition, whether it's government-funded or through a private bank. Although taking out a loan means dealing with those pesky interest fees, it can also be a viable way to make your study abroad dreams a reality.

Apply for Scholarships

Free money to study abroad? We'll take it. There are tons of online databases that have scholarships available specifically for students who are studying abroad. You can research scholarships for your specific country, program, or area of study. Additionally, many study abroad program providers also offer scholarships to students who are participating in one of their programs.

One of the best study abroad grants out there is the Benjamin A. Gilman International Scholarship, which is very competitive but offers scholarships of up to $5,000. More than 2,300 scholarships are awarded through the program each year, and the average award amount is $4,000. If you receive a Pell Grant or will be receiving one at the time of your study abroad program, this scholarship is definitely worth a shot.

Your school can also be a valuable resource when you're searching for study abroad scholarships. Grants offered through your university will usually be easier to get, given the smaller number of applicants. A quick visit to the study abroad office is a great way to find out about school-specific scholarships, as well as other outside resources. Your school's study abroad website will likely have a list of all the available scholarships as well as information about how to contact a study abroad advisor and find the study abroad office on campus. Be sure to check out academic department scholarships as well, as you may be eligible for aid based on your major.

Make sure to start your research early, though, because study abroad scholarships for the coming year often have early deadlines!

In general, spring program deadlines fall during September and October, while autumn program deadlines are in March and April.

HOW TO PREPARE FOR YOUR TIME ABROAD

You've done your research, asked all of the questions, and finally found the perfect program for you. But in between stalking Facebook photos of former participants and dreaming about the amazing sites and cities you'll visit, reality has probably started to set in: How do you get a visa? Where do you live? How do you pack for five months in only two suitcases?!

Fret not, collegiette. There are tons of resources available to help you prepare for your study abroad experience and nail down all the details so you can hop on that plane excited and ready to explore!

Learn about the Experiences of Previous Study Abroad Students

One of the best ways to learn about what to expect when abroad is by speaking with people who have already gone on the programs you're considering. If you don't know anyone who has studied abroad with your program options, your study abroad program advisor may be able to connect you with the right students.

Attend Orientation for Your Program

Most study abroad offices will hold informational onboarding sessions on campus for the students traveling as part of the same program. It's very helpful to meet other program participants early so that you can arrange your travel schedules together and know who else will be on your trip. If you're traveling through an external program, try to connect with your future travel buddies online.

Apply for a Student Visa

A visa is a temporary government document that allows you to remain in the country you're traveling to for a specific period of time. Some countries do not require a visa if you will be there for fewer than a certain number of days, and others will require very specific dates for your entry and departure from their country. Because the visa process is full of exceptions, it's best to check with your study abroad country's consulate to see if you need a visa, and if you do, how to get one. The visa process can take months, so be sure to get going on this early!

Finances, Changing Money, and ATMs

If you head abroad and make charges on your credit card without notifying a representative at your bank first, your credit card will likely be canceled because your bank will think your card has been stolen. Let your bank know the exact dates when you will be traveling abroad and the countries you may visit while you're there. Also ask your bank if they have any international partner banks whose ATMs you can use while abroad to avoid getting charged any nasty fees. Finally, do yourself a favor and exchange some cash at the airport before you leave. Make sure to have enough cash for a few days to pay for any taxis, food, or other fees you might need to cover as you get acclimated.

Medications, Vaccinations, and Health Insurance

One of the most important people to contact before studying abroad is your doctor. If you regularly take medication, you should ask her if you can get a prescription for enough of the medication to last your entire trip. You should also ask her whether you are up to date on all of your immunizations and see if she recommends getting any additional vaccinations before your trip. You can also talk to a representative at the embassy of the country that you are visiting, or consult the Centers for Disease Control and Prevention for further vaccination recommendations.

Set Up Communication Solutions

If you don't have a phone you want to bring, find out the best option for getting a phone in your new country. The most cost-effective option will probably be to purchase a pay-as-you-go phone so that you can add credit to make phone calls and text as necessary.

Additionally, don't forget about Skype and Google Hangouts. Just make sure to let family and friends know what the time difference is so that your grandmother doesn't try to Skype you at 3 A.M. your time!

Make a Study Abroad Adventure List!

To make the most of all your excursions, create an adventure list! Figuring out what your top things to do are before you leave will make planning your trips once you're abroad a lot less stressful.

Not sure of your destination's must-sees? Guidebooks, travel blogs, and plain old Google searches will yield lists—and lists and lists and lists—of every hot spot. Also, ask your friends and family about places they've traveled to and their recommendations. Their firsthand experiences will be invaluable. Happy traveling, collegiettes!

Converters and Adapters

There are two options when it comes to making sure your beloved electronic devices work: adapter plugs and voltage converters. Adapters take the shape of the plug. You simply plug the adapter into the wall, and then plug your appliance into the adapter—just make sure your electronic device can handle the voltage that the country uses. On the other hand, a converter changes the voltage, because countries abroad use different quantities of voltage. You might find it useful to wait until you reach your destination to purchase any hair dryers, straighteners, or curling irons so that you can ensure they'll work! Not only will you save space packing, but you also won't risk frying your appliances . . . and potentially burning down the building.

STAYING SAFE ABROAD

One of the perks of studying abroad, aside from having the opportunity to live in a foreign country, is having the freedom to be able to travel. As exciting as traveling may be, though, you can only truly appreciate a new environment if you feel safe in it. Before you go anywhere, follow these steps and take note of these suggestions to make sure that you're fully informed about your destination and prepared for whatever circumstances may arise.

What to Consider When Booking a Hostel

Read reviews of your accommodation before booking and make sure the reviews say that the hostel feels safe and is up to a standard of cleanliness. Make note of the hostel's operating hours. Hostels often do not have a reception desk or a concierge, meaning that— you guessed it—they aren't open 24/7. If you end up locked out in a sketchy area, your safety could be jeopardized.

What to Bring with You and How to Plan for Your Travels

You'll need to pack more than chic outfits for your weekend getaway to Paris. Make photocopies of your important documents! The State Department has a useful website on safe travel for study abroad students that's definitely worth taking a look at before you go off on your adventures.

Documents to make copies of include:

- Your passport identification page
- Airline tickets

- Driver's license
- Credit cards
- Serial numbers of your travelers' checks
- Insurance information
- Addresses and phone numbers of places you're staying

Making these photocopies is not the only crucial step you need to take to ensure that you have all of your bases covered, though—you also have to make sure that your family and friends have copies in case of an emergency. Make enough copies so that you, too, can have copies with you on your travels. Remember: Keep the photocopies separate from the originals, so that if you lose your bag or have any of the originals stolen, you'll have something to fall back on.

Familiarize yourself with the local customs and laws of your destination. Nothing is worse than embodying the stereotype of the ignorant American by offending the locals. Observing local customs can be just as crucial as local laws in terms of safety. Some things that are deemed appropriate or normal in the United States might be considered provocative or even illegal in other countries. Make sure to research the customs of the country you're visiting before you decide what to pack.

If you'll be traveling to a non-English-speaking country, look up important phrases beforehand. Many major cities, especially in Europe, are filled with English speakers, but relying on this will make you extremely vulnerable if you find yourself in a situation where you are unable to communicate with people. Pick up a mini dictionary or download a dictionary app to your smartphone for quick reference! Before you travel, create a list of common phrases to keep with you at all times so that you'll be much better equipped to communicate with natives.

Five Tips for Staying Safe in Foreign Cities

Keep in mind that you're not just taking a fun trip with your friends—you're also entering into a foreign country. You can't expect to be able to simply show up and figure things out from there—if you do, you could unknowingly put yourself and whomever you're traveling with in unpredictable, dangerous, or even life-threatening situations. Heed these tips to stay safe.

- Pick up city and public transportation maps from your destination's airport or train station.
- Take out money in the local currency as soon as possible! If your credit card is stolen or lost while you're there, you need to make sure that you still have enough money with you to cover your expenses.
- Beware of pickpockets and keep your belongings close to your person. Get a money pouch, which sits against your body, under your clothing, and out of sight from pickpockets.
- Keep all crucial contact information on your body at all times: Write down the local emergency phone number (911 only works in the U.S.!), your hostel's address and phone number, and anything else that might be pertinent in an emergency situation.
- Make sure that your family and friends have a way to reach you and that you have a way to reach them, and, especially if you're traveling alone, be sure to communicate with them regularly so they know where you are and that you're safe.

Wellness Check-In: Five Things to Pack to Stay Safe While Studying Abroad

1. Copies of your passport identification page, license, visa, and other important documents
2. Prescription medications or other medical necessities (e.g., aspirin, bandages, and cold/flu medicine)
3. Mini dictionaries for any language you know you'll need to speak during your travels
4. Health insurance card and other identification documents
5. Cash in the foreign currency

Chapter Checklist

✓ Talk to your study abroad advisor to learn everything you need for your big trip.

✓ Meet with your academic advisor about major requirements.

✓ Research programs and attend informational sessions so you can decide on the best program for you.

✓ Make a list of your study abroad goals and travel plans to make sure you get the most out of your trip.

✓ Choose a study abroad location based on the experience you want to have—not just what your friends are doing!

✓ Set up meetings with your study abroad advisor to learn everything you'll need to know.

✓ Consult your parents, financial advisor, and financial aid office to determine how you'll pay for your time abroad.

✓ Research the requirements for a visa and apply well in advance.

✓ Prepare and make copies of all of the necessary documents and information you might need.

✓ Pack up your suitcases (and then take 50 percent out—we promise, you won't need ten pairs of jeans).

✓ Make amazing memories during your time abroad!

PART 2

Staying Healthy on Campus

S leep eight hours a night. Eat your greens. Get in some gym time. You've heard so many things about what it takes to stay healthy, and while all these things are true when it comes to your health, there's a lot more you need to know to get through college in tip-top shape.

Do you know the difference between being stressed and being too stressed? How do you know when your drinking is a problem? Did you know there's such a thing as too much exercise? Is it even possible to eat healthy in the dining hall? When is it okay to nap? And what in the world can you expect when you visit your gynecologist? We'll answer all these questions and more in the next few chapters—you'll walk away knowing everything it takes to stay healthy (you just might give those pre-med students a run for their money!), and most importantly, where to get professional and medical help for yourself or a friend if you need it.

CHAPTER 5

Nutrition, Fitness, and Eating Disorders

Staying healthy in college is a mix of having a balanced diet and exercising regularly—and we're fully aware that maintaining all that with a full class load, a packed social schedule, and everything else that college comes with is much easier said than done. Getting into these habits as soon as you get to campus will make a healthy lifestyle easier to come by than if you have to change old habits first. We'll start with everything you need to know about eating well at school.

WHERE TO EAT ON CAMPUS

Every college campus is going to have a standard dining hall. Usually set up like a cafeteria, it'll include several stations featuring different kinds of food. The dining hall is generally where you'll go if you have a meal plan.

You might find another dining area that's set up with vendors and traditional chain restaurants. Keep in mind that you may not be able to use your meal plan to eat at these restaurants, so you should be prepared to spend your own money at these locations.

Most campuses will also have a café or coffee shop (such as Starbucks, or maybe an independently run shop). Whether you can use your meal plan there depends on whether it's a chain or a school-owned location.

Many dorm buildings will have their own dining areas, too. Especially if the dorm is a small trek away from the main campus, there is likely to be a grab-and-go or convenience shop in the building, or a dining area that's kind of like a smaller version of the dining hall.

Your campus may also have a small grocery or convenience store. If you're lucky enough to have access to one, take advantage of it! You can be more in control of what you're eating if you're able to go grocery shopping more often. Take the opportunity to stock up on fresh fruit and veggies and other food that you can keep in your dorm room.

What to Do If You're Fed Up with the Food on Campus

When you've been eating in the same places every day for months, you'll probably get bored with your meals. What you might not know is that there are likely lots of other on-campus dining areas that you don't know of yet that might even accept your meal plan! If your college is a part of a larger university with grad or pre-professional schools, each of these locations might have its own café, deli, or other places to eat. Check out what's available at the law school or the business school, and you might find some new options. Or, if your campus is home to buildings and amenities that are open to the public, there might be an on-premises restaurant, such as at a museum or exhibition space.

HOW TO EAT HEALTHY IN THE DINING HALL

Gooey macaroni and cheese. Juicy steaks. Warm fudge brownies. All in limitless portions. Do you want fries with that?

Love it or hate it, you're going to be spending a lot of time in the campus dining hall, and you're going to have to get used to eating healthy there, too. Stick to these tips.

Don't Avoid the Fat

Adding a little fat to your meal will help you stay full longer. What you should be avoiding is saturated fat; get your fats from healthy fat sources like nuts, fish, and plant oils instead.

Mix and Match

Just because most dining halls have specific stations doesn't mean you can't get creative! Grab some grilled chicken at the burger station and pair it with some marinara sauce at the pasta station. You'll get a more varied diet, and it just might taste better than your typical dining hall meal!

Go Online

Most colleges will post their menus for the day online, and if you're lucky, they'll post the calorie counts, too. This gives you the opportunity to plan your meals so you can decide whether you want to splurge on that ice cream for lunch or if you want to save your calories for chocolate mousse at dinner.

Bring Your Own Extras

The truth is, your dining hall isn't going to have everything you want—and it's not going to have the healthiest options, either. Incorporate some of your own add-ons! Bring hummus to eat your carrots with rather than the ranch in the dining hall, or even spices to dress up chicken so you're not tempted to dip it into gravy.

Eat Your Eggs!

Protein keeps your blood sugar levels more stable, and you'll stay full for longer—so when you're choosing between a bagel or eggs for breakfast, opt for the latter.

Stay Fresh

That glass of OJ sure feels like a hefty serving of fruit, but you're probably just getting a lot of water and sugar (and not the good kind). Instead, go for the real thing when it comes to fruits and veggies!

Let Yourself Splurge!

Nobody was made to be perfect, so give yourself a break. A healthy diet is all about balance, so instead of binge eating chocolate-chip cookies after denying yourself the privilege for weeks, treat yourself every now and then so you don't go into craving overload.

Seven Ways to Energize Without Coffee

You know you're not supposed to have caffeine too late in the day, but it's 3 P.M. and you can hardly stop your head from hitting the desk in your history class. Sound familiar? Instead of reaching for that cup of coffee, try these seven things instead:

- **Have a protein-filled snack.** Try any of the protein-based snacks mentioned in the next section. The protein will give your body a boost to help you get through the rest of your day, without getting in the way of your bedtime later on.
- **Take your vitamins.** In this case, you'll want to take vita-min B (usually found in animal products such as meat,

poultry, dairy, and fish). Fatigue, poor concentration, anxiety, and depression are linked to a vitamin B deficiency, so taking a B complex supplement regularly may help bring your energy up.

- **Try a quick workout.** We know—when you're tired, going to the gym is the last thing on your mind. But even a short session on the treadmill with your favorite tunes blasting can kick up your energy levels for the rest of the day. Just be sure you're not doing this too soon before you go to sleep!
- **Take a cold shower.** The temperature will stimulate your system and speed up circulation, which will make you more alert.
- **Take a walk.** If you're nodding off in class, excuse yourself and take a quick walk down the hall. It'll have a similar effect to working out, and will keep you awake for the rest of that lecture.
- **Meditate.** It's a tool used to help you relax and fall asleep, but that relaxation can also clear your mind and bring you an increased sense of mental and physical awareness. In short, you'll be much more alert.

HEALTHY FOODS TO KEEP IN YOUR DORM ROOM

Now that you've mastered what to pick and what to skip in the dining hall, you need to know how to eat well at home, too. There will be times when the dining locations on campus are closed, or when you just don't feel like having cafeteria food for the millionth time. That's why it's key to have healthy building blocks for meals in your dorm room. Hang on to this collegiette-budget-friendly shopping list— you'll get the most bang for your buck and you'll stay healthy, too.

- Oatmeal
- Eggs

- Rice
- Beans
- Granola
- In-season fruits and veggies
- Green tea
- Tortilla chips and salsa

EATING HEALTHY ON THE GO

You're probably spending most of your day on campus, going from classes to study sessions to office hours. And with such a busy schedule, you don't have time to sit down for a decent meal every single day. You'll need to plan for days like this so you're not skipping meals or grabbing something quick from a vending machine that probably will have little to no nutritional value. We've got you covered from day to night with quick and easy foods that you can pack with you or grab on the way to your next discussion group!

Breakfast

You've already heard that breakfast is the most important meal of the day—it affects your metabolism, your energy levels, and your mental abilities throughout the day. But you ask yourself: Is it worth losing that extra hour of sleep for? Fortunately, you don't have to give up one for the other. You can grab breakfast (and lunch, and a ton of snacks, too!) on the go without sacrificing your beauty sleep or your health. Here's the proof:

Greek Yogurt

One serving-size container of Greek yogurt contains anywhere from ten to twenty grams of protein, which is around ¼ to ⅓ of the amount of protein you should be getting each day. Getting protein first thing in the morning will help energize your body, which has essentially been fasting for the past eight to ten hours since last night's dinner.

Banana and Skim Milk Smoothie

Crafting up this drink will take you all of five seconds—throw a banana, some skim milk, and a pinch of cinnamon into a personal blender, and you've just made yourself a wholesome breakfast that you can sip on your way to class! You'll be getting tons of vitamins and minerals, plus a good deal of calcium and potassium to keep you strong and healthy.

Whole-Wheat English Muffin

Pop this baby in the toaster, spread some peanut butter on it, and you'll be getting your day started with a good source of fiber and a touch of protein.

Lunch

If you're caught in a bind, here are some quick, healthy, and surprisingly filling alternatives that will hold you over until you do have time to get a full meal.

Fruit with Two Tablespoons of Peanut Butter

Choose a pear, apple, or banana and pick up some single serving peanut butter or almond butter tubes. Top it off with a handful of whole-wheat crackers.

Tuna Pouch with Pita

Super portable and super filling, a whole wheat pita and a single-serve pouch of tuna (they even make them in tons of different flavors!) will deliver the fiber to keep you satiated and omega-three fatty acids for a healthy heart.

Snacking Between Classes

Staying fueled throughout the day requires a little something-something between your major meals. We're all for guilty pleasures, but set the mini cupcakes aside for now—here's what you really need to snack smart:

Mixed Nuts

They're full of fat and protein, both of which will keep you full longer, so you won't be snacking on these and then raiding your fridge again an hour later.

Sliced Apples and Peanut Butter

We've already pointed out peanut butter as a filling addition to any meal or snack. It's made with the good kind of fat (the kind you need to survive!) and packs in some protein, too. Add an apple for extra fiber!

WORKING OUT ON CAMPUS

You already know that for your overall health and well-being, maintaining a good diet is only half the battle. You'll also need to exercise to keep your body in shape. Getting exercise isn't just about achieving that perfect bikini bod for spring break; it's beneficial for your mental health, too. So, you're ready to hit the ground running (or walking) at school. But where do you even begin?

The Campus Gym

Every college campus will have a full-service gym, full of all the usual suspects (treadmills, ellipticals, rowing machines, free weights, and more). If you're lucky, you'll find a bunch of other amenities, too: basketball and tennis courts, a lap pool, a climbing wall, an outdoor track and field, a dance studio, and more. You'll want to take full advantage of free gym access while you can these four years (once you leave school, gym memberships to such well-equipped locations could be hundreds of dollars per month!). Some gyms on campus will also offer group fitness classes. Depending on your school, they might be included in your gym membership or you might have to pay for classes separately (typically they're priced relatively low). Try a new yoga class or get your friends together for Zumba!

P.E. Classes

That's right—gym class isn't just for high schoolers. If you're trying to learn a new sport or if you know you're not going to make it to the gym regularly without some sort of consequences to motivate you, sign up for a class! Try something new with a modern dance class, or do what you already know, such as a spinning class. It's also a great way of meeting people who may be interested in the same type of exercise as you, so that once the class is over, you'll have found a new gym buddy!

Intramural Sports

If you played sports in high school and are looking to continue doing so in college, but aren't serious enough to join one of your school's competitive teams, look into intramural sports teams on campus. Usually it's an open environment that accepts people of all levels, so even if you're nowhere near a pro soccer player, you'll still be welcome to join the team! It's more about having fun and getting in exercise rather than about winning games (though you'll have plenty of chances to do that, too). You can probably find information on these teams on your campus gym's website, the flyer board at the gym or in your dorm, or over mailing list servers.

Running Clubs

Can't seem to get your friends to join you on a run, but don't want to run alone? Look into whether there's a running club at your school (and if there isn't, you should think about starting one!). These groups usually meet several times a week, although you can choose how often you run with the club.

Dorm Room Workouts

Sorry, but the "it's too cold to go to the gym!" excuse no longer applies—believe it or not, you *can* get in a full-body workout in the 100 square feet that is your dorm room. Look up workout videos online, or craft your own workout routine using tried-and-true moves like crunches, push-ups, tricep dips, planks, lunges, squats, and more. There's a lot you can do with just your own body weight, but you can also get tools like small hand and ankle weights, a resistance band, or even a small stool to help supplement your workout.

Working Out While You're Studying

So you might not be doing any heavy cardio while you're sitting at your desk, but you can do a few moves that activate different muscle groups without ever getting up.

- **Straight posture:** First and foremost, sit up straight and maintain a good posture; this alone keeps your abs active. While you're there, squeeze and release your abdominal muscles during the course of your study session.
- **Glute squeeze:** Inconspicuous enough even to do in class, these will let you work all day towards that firm butt. Squeeze your gluteal muscles as hard as you can, hold for ten seconds, and release.
- **Calf raises:** Place both feet flat on the ground. Alternating feet, lift your heels up and down in a slow controlled motion, keeping your toes on the floor.
- **Trapezius squeeze:** Bend your elbows slightly, and pull them back, pinching your shoulder blades together.

EATING DISORDERS IN COLLEGE

It can almost seem as if having a healthy lifestyle is all about control and restrictions. If this is the first thing that comes to mind, it's time to change that dangerous perception. Staying fit and healthy isn't about withholding—it's about finding a good balance. When you focus too hard on the rights and wrongs (such as writing down everything you eat to manage your intake down to the exact number of calories you're consuming), you could be starting to step into some pretty risky territory.

So are you living healthily, or do you have an unhealthy obsession? We're going to go over some of the most common eating disorders and how they affect collegiettes.

Anorexia and Bulimia

College women are especially susceptible to developing eating disorders such as anorexia and bulimia. Full-blown eating disorders generally happen between the ages of eighteen and twenty-one—as in, right during your college years. Anorexia is when you severely limit your food intake, and, despite being underweight, have a distorted view of your own body and will continue to diet. Bulimia generally functions through a system of bingeing and purging—you'll eat and then force the food out of your body either through the use of laxatives or by making yourself throw up after meals.

Binge Eating Disorder

Then there's the opposite: Overeating. Binge eating is considered an eating disorder, but it can often be disregarded as purely an issue of poor self-restraint, which is one reason many people don't know to get help for it. It can happen based on your emotional state; maybe eating brings you comfort. Or it can happen as a result of too many dietary restrictions; if you aren't eating enough, your body will naturally crave the nutrients and may lead you to binge, before starting the cycle of dieting again after a bingeing episode. Aside from weight gain and all of the health problems that come with it, binge eating is also associated with acid reflux disease, insulin surges that lead to diabetes, and other long-term effects.

Are You Stress Eating?

Often, you might be eating as a result of stress and not even know it. To determine if it might be affecting you, observe your eating patterns. Is there a specific place or situation (such as a study session) that makes you want to reach for food? Do you eat when you're bored? Ask yourself what's triggering your eating if you turn to food to bring you comfort. And the next time you're digging around for something to eat, ask yourself, "Am I really hungry?" The best time to eat is when your stomach feels empty (but isn't hurting with hunger pangs).

Over-Exercising

There's often a lot of discussion on how to eat healthy, but how much you exercise can be overlooked. How much is too much? Addiction to exercise is a real condition. You find yourself scheduling your days around going to the gym, and the minute you eat a meal, you have an urge to work those calories off.

Too much exercise without proper rest periods in between can, in the short term, weaken your immune system because you're not giving your body the time it needs to recover—and the more you work out, the more time your muscles actually need to recover. Too much exercise can also affect you emotionally and cause changes in your behavior: When you over-train, your body releases a hormone called cortisol, the same hormone that's released when you're stressed. In the long term, over-exercising can set you up for serious injuries that may cause permanent damage, depending on the type of workout you're doing and where you're putting the most strain on your body. You could also be burning way more calories than is healthy, which could lead to malnourishment.

What to Do If You or a Friend Has an Eating Disorder

It can be hard to spot eating disorders in their early stages; the obvious signs aren't always evident immediately. Here are subtle signs of an eating disorder to look out for:

- Obsession with calories, food, or nutrition
- Compulsive exercising
- Making excuses to get out of eating
- Avoiding social situations that involve food
- Eating alone, at night, or in secret

If you or a friend is suffering from an eating disorder, here are several resources available both on and off campus.

Student Health Center

The student health center will have the tools to make sure you're physically stable, or they'll run any necessary tests (blood and urine tests, a thyroid screening, etc.) to get an overall look at how your body is functioning. If it's an extreme case, they'll likely refer you to a local (or the university) hospital, and they'll be able to direct you to counseling centers on campus.

Eating Disorder Specialists on Campus

Many colleges are being more proactive about making sure resources are directly available to students. You may have centers or organizations on campus dedicated to eating disorders and related issues where you'll find counselors who are trained to deal with eating disorders.

Dietitian

If you are having a difficult time with food but don't necessarily have a classifiable eating disorder, you should meet with a dietitian who can help go over a meal plan that makes sense for you. A dietitian will give you the tools to maintain a healthy lifestyle without going overboard. And though dietitians aren't therapists, they may have the knowledge and training to at least help you talk through how to have a good relationship with food.

The National Eating Disorders Association (www.nationaleatingdisorders.org)

The NEDA is the ultimate resource for all things associated with eating disorders. They have a confidential helpline (1-800-931-2237; find more hotlines at the end of this section!) where you can speak with volunteers who are there just to talk to you, or who can point you to resources in your area. Or, use their search function to find therapists and psychiatrists around you, especially if the resources on your campus aren't sufficient.

www.MyBodyScreening.org

From Screening for Mental Health, Inc., this online screening tool is a free assessment you can take to gauge your risk of an eating disorder. There's an assessment geared specifically for college students, too, and after completion, you'll receive a list of resources and other tools to help you take next steps.

National Hotlines
- National Association of Anorexia Nervosa and Associated Disorders: 630-577-1330 (*www.anad.org*)
- The Renfrew Center (eating disorder specialist referrals): 1-800-RENFREW (1-800-736-3739) (*www.renfrewcenter.com*)
- Bulimia and Self-Help Hotline: 314-588-1683
- Overeaters Anonymous: 505-891-2664 (*www.oa.org*)

Wellness Check-In: Six Workout Mistakes to Avoid

1. You forget to warm up. Jumping right into a workout means you haven't given your body the time to get adequate oxygen and blood flow to the muscles you're using, increasing your risk of injury. Start with a few minutes of walking to get your blood flowing!

2. You do tons of reps . . . but have terrible form. If you're not doing your exercises with the right form, you could be doing worse than nothing for your body—you could be hurting yourself. Ask a trainer at the gym to show you how to do a move correctly if you're unsure.

3. You study or watch TV while you're on the elliptical. If your mind isn't in the workout, you might not actually be giving it your all. Being conscious of your body while you're exercising will help you concentrate on picking up the pace, maintaining the correct posture, and breathing right.

4. You speed through your weights. Doing each repetition too quickly only means you're not getting the full benefit of the workout. Lift the weight slowly as you breathe in, hold for a moment at the height of the contraction, and then exhale as you release, paying attention to the resistance.

5. You don't drink enough water. Hydrate with one to two cups of water before you exercise, and then continue to drink during your workout (don't guzzle it down, otherwise you'll give yourself cramps!). Without water, you and your muscles become dehydrated, so you won't be able to work to your fullest potential.

6. You're on the elliptical for an hour every day. As you repeat the same workout each day, your body is adapting to those steps. At a certain point, you're no longer progressing, so instead of getting back on the same machine for the millionth time, switch up what you're doing at the gym each time you go.

Chapter Checklist

✓ Maintaining a healthy lifestyle means making good diet and exercise a habit! Eat on a regular schedule (within one hour of waking up, and every three to four hours from there) and make gym time a regular part of your day.

✓ Don't forget to eat breakfast (or lunch, or dinner). Skipping meals should never be an option, but know what quick snacks are available to keep you well fueled until you can have an appropriate meal.

✓ Keep unhealthy snacks out of your dorm room. When potato chips and gummy bears are within arm's reach, you're making it too easy to dine on junk food. Avoid temptation altogether!

✓ No more excuses: With so many workout options available on campus (including those in your own dorm room!), stop telling yourself you'll get to the gym tomorrow. Today is the day, so make it happen.

✓ Know the difference between a healthy lifestyle and when obsession over diet or fitness becomes a problem. Know where to get help when you need it.

CHAPTER 6

Physical Health

Staying home sick in college is a little different from staying home sick when you're, well, at home. Since you're totally on your own, even when you feel like you're on your deathbed, you still have to do everything yourself—that's right, you won't have anybody to bring you hot tea or a steaming bowl of chicken noodle soup. In short, getting sick at school sucks, so you want to avoid it as much as possible. But how do you do that when being on campus is kind of like living in one gigantic petri dish? We're here to tell you!

GETTING ENOUGH SLEEP

As much as it's drilled into our heads that getting enough sleep is vital to our mental and physical health, it isn't always a priority for collegiettes. There are papers to write, tests to cram for, social lives to be had—who has time for sleep, anyway?

Well, beyond feeling tired, there are a number of consequences to not catching enough Zs. In the short term, you'll experience decreased alertness (ever find yourself nodding off in class?) or memory impairment (you may have a hard time remembering those extra chapters you stayed up late reading). In the long term, you're putting yourself at greater risk for high blood pressure, heart attacks, diabetes, and other illnesses. Obesity is linked to lack of sleep, which disrupts appetite-suppressing hormones, as are early signs of aging, since your body won't produce as much of the reparative growth hormones and collagen you need—talk about beauty sleep!

And of course, there's your immune system. Not getting enough sleep can lower your resistance to viruses and bacteria in both the short and long term. That means whether you're pulling a few all-nighters to study during exam period or you're cutting into sleep pretty much every night of the semester, you're more likely to catch whatever bug is making the rounds on campus.

How to Nap the Right Way

Late afternoon hits, and you're not sure if you can make it the rest of the day—your eyelids are drooping and you feel ready to pass out. You succumb to sleep, and next thing you know you're getting up at 7 P.M. and you won't be able to fall asleep for another several hours. So how do you nap without disrupting your sleep schedule?

- Plan naps on days you're going to stay up late, instead of napping to make up for a late night after it's already happened.
- Naps should only be twenty to thirty minutes each. Your sleep cycle consists of five stages, and when you nap, you don't want to enter the deeper stages of sleep. A short nap will only hit the first or second stage, so when you wake up, you won't be tired from interrupting a deep slumber, but energized.
- Afraid you won't be able to get up in that short a period? Try drinking a cup of coffee (leave out the heavy cream and packets of sugar!) before your nap; by the time you get up, the caffeine will have kicked in and you'll feel much more awake. Don't make a habit of using caffeine as an aid, though—this method is for emergencies only!

So how *do* you get more sleep with a collegiette's busy schedule? Follow these seven tips and you're guaranteed to sleep better tonight—and the rest of the semester.

Go to Bed and Get Up at the Same Time Every Day

Even if you have a morning lecture one day and a class that doesn't start until afternoon the next, don't do an early A.M. wakeup call for that lecture and then sleep in before your later class; doing so will only confuse your sleep patterns, and you'll have trouble falling asleep and waking up when you're supposed to. But what about the weekends? There *is* a one- to two-hour period of flexibility, so if you're going out on the weekends or sleeping in just a little some days, you'll still be okay.

Have Some Downtime Before Bed

No, this doesn't mean spending three hours watching *Real Housewives* reruns before it's time to go to sleep (even artificial light can affect your internal clock—this goes for your phone, too!). Instead, take a hot bath or snuggle into bed with a magazine; make these relaxing activities a daily ritual, and they'll start to signal to your body that it's time to shut down.

Don't Drink Caffeine after Noon

You already know that a cup of coffee will boost your alertness and adrenaline (it's why we drink it!) but having it too late in the day may keep you going for long after you should've been asleep. Depending on your body's tolerance, even having caffeine early in the day can affect how well you sleep at night.

Your Bed Is for Sleep Only!

Don't eat Chinese takeout and watch your favorite Netflix show in bed or do any studying there. You need to associate your bed with sleep, not daytime activities.

Get Exercise at the Right Times

Even half an hour of exercise in the morning (or later in the day, if you're not a morning person) can help you snooze at night. Just don't hit the treadmill right before bedtime—working out will energize you, so make sure you're getting to the gym several hours before you go to bed.

Watch What You Eat Before Bed

Avoid high-fat, heavy, and spicy foods; they're more likely to cause indigestion, which will leave you unable to sleep. If you're hungry, you can have a carb-filled snack (don't hate on the carbs!), like saltines or pretzels—the high glycemic index may speed up the release of brain chemicals that promote sleep.

Relax

You know the feeling—it's well past midnight during a weeknight and you *still* can't sleep. You start stressing about sleeping in the next morning, or being too tired to get through the day—which causes you to toss and turn even more. Instead of looking at your phone every thirty seconds to make sure your alarm is on or to check what time it is, grab a book or a magazine or try meditating.

HOW TO AVOID GETTING SICK

Even if you've reached the gold standard of sleep and are getting your eight hours every night, when you're living in close quarters with hundreds of other college students (after all, your roommate sleeps three feet from you!), you're bound to be exposed to something infectious. We're going to say it now: You're *going* to get sick in college. To some degree, it's unavoidable. But there are steps you can take to make it happen as infrequently as possible. We'll go over some of the most common illnesses floating around college campuses, including how to avoid them and how to treat them.

Flu

High fever, coughing, congestion—sounds like flu season. Getting your flu vaccine each year is your most effective way of combating this highly infectious illness. You can get vaccinated at your student health center or at most drugstores. Even if you've been vaccinated, be sure to wash your hands often and carry hand sanitizer.

Already sick with the flu? Rest up and drink lots of water. Most over-the-counter medicines, such as ibuprofen and decongestants, will help relieve your symptoms while you're recovering. The flu is a viral infection, so antibiotics (used to treat bacterial infections) won't have an effect on it. If your symptoms are too much to handle, your doctor can prescribe you antiviral medications to help (usually given to young children or seniors who are at risk for complications), but for the most part, the recovery process just requires time and some rest and recuperation.

Mono

Short for "mononucleosis" and otherwise known as the "kissing disease," mono is transmitted through saliva—kissing, sharing drinks or utensils, or even sneezing and coughing can pass this illness along. If you know someone who has (or had—a person can be a carrier even months after their symptoms are gone) mono, avoid any situation in which you might swap saliva, including touching hands; your friend may have touched her hand to her mouth, and you might touch your hand to your mouth.

If you get mono, you might be out of school for a week or two, depending on how severe your case is. Watch for fatigue, fever, headache, swollen tonsils and lymph nodes, a sore throat, and/or a loss of appetite for an extended period of time. Avoid too much movement during this time, as your spleen is likely swollen and at risk of rupturing. Since mono is also a viral infection, antibiotics won't be of any use here, and the best treatment is lots of rest and plenty of fluids—but definitely see your doctor if you think you have mono so that he or she can set you up on the best treatment plan.

Conjunctivitis

Better known as pinkeye, this condition will leave your eyes looking bloodshot and watery and producing discharge. It can be viral (more commonly you'll wake up with crusting and discharge, but throughout the day your eyes are more watery) or bacterial (producing thicker yellow discharge throughout the day).

The best way to keep from getting pinkeye is to wash your hands frequently, especially if you know it's been going around campus or if you know somebody who's infected.

Pinkeye generally disappears on its own within a few days, but because it's so uncomfortable, you should visit a doctor for eye drops—and to make sure it's not a bacterial infection, in which case you'd need an antibiotic eye drop. And make sure you're washing your hands often, most importantly after every time you touch your eyes! Pinkeye spreads like wildfire, so it's important to try to keep it contained if you catch it.

Meningitis

Though rare, meningitis can happen, and it can cause a lot of damage. There are two types of meningitis, viral and bacterial. Viral meningitis is typically not a big deal, but bacterial meningitis can be deadly if not treated right away. It's extremely contagious and can be spread through close contact, and the most telling symptoms are headache, fever, and a stiff neck, although symptoms can also closely mirror those of the flu.

If you suspect you might have meningitis, see a doctor right away—early detection is vital if you have bacterial meningitis. You'll be put on antibiotics if it's bacterial, and if it's viral, rest and hydration will usually help the sickness pass, though your doctor may prescribe you antiviral medication as well.

Take a Multivitamin

Multivitamins are exactly what they sound like: nutritional supplements that contain a mix of vitamins and minerals, called micronutrients. Because your body requires vitamins and minerals to survive, there isn't any one thing that multivitamins benefit; they generally supplement your overall health. Multivitamins are especially important for vegetarians and others with dietary restrictions that may cause them to not take in all the vitamins a person needs. It never hurts to take a multivitamin in addition to what you're getting through your food. They shouldn't be replacing anything in your diet, however, so don't think you can eat anything you want once you start taking a multivitamin!

The key takeaway from all of this? You can never wash your hands too often, especially before eating; avoid sharing things when there's a chance of transferring bodily fluids—utensils, hand towels, even makeup; and be sure you're up to date on all your shots (most colleges will require a certain set of vaccinations before you're even allowed on campus).

WHERE TO GO WHEN YOU GET SICK

You've probably diagnosed yourself based on what you've read on WebMD—but though the Internet can be helpful when you're trying to make sense of your symptoms, if there's anything you have questions about or if you have symptoms that persist no matter what you do, you need to see your doctor. And when you're on campus, that's the student health center. Before you arrived on campus, your college likely required you to join the health insurance plan provided by the school. A visit to the center will come at little or no cost to insured students. The student health center will provide services you'd expect to see at any doctor's office: You'll go for annuals, physicals, women's health issues (more on this in Chapter

9), vaccinations, illnesses, and more. Most operate by appointment, but many will also take walk-ins (if not anytime, then during certain days or hours). Many will provide counseling and therapy as well, or at least be able to refer you to these and other specialty services you might need.

Since student health centers are generally clinics, they'll likely need to refer you to the local hospital for any extensive testing (if you need an MRI, for example). You'll also find yourself in the hospital if you need in-patient treatment or any major operation, but for the most part, the student health center is the best place for you to start.

You already know the obvious signs that you should visit the doctor, but there may be some health concerns you're not taking seriously enough. Here are some symptoms that you might need to get checked out:

You Get Terrible Headaches

Everybody will get a headache from time to time, but it's not normal if the pain is excruciating, if the headaches are frequent, or if the headaches are causing visual distortion or feelings of weakness in your arms and face.

You Have Never-Ending Exhaustion

It's college—being tired is a part of a collegiette's job description. But if you're tired no matter how much sleep you get, or if your sleep patterns and even your mood are affected by your exhaustion, a doctor may be able to find out whether there's anything else causing the symptom.

You're Over- or Undereating

If your appetite changes drastically, it could be a sign of mental and/or physical illness such as depression, extreme stress, gastrointestinal tract issues, a stomach virus, or something else.

Get checked out if your appetite or your weight fluctuates without explanation.

Trust your instincts. You know your body best, so if anything feels off, it doesn't hurt to make an appointment. After all, you're better off safe than sorry!

You Have Irregular Periods

There's a lot that can change your menstrual cycle (stress, diet, etc.), but sudden changes could be signs of a thyroid or hormonal problem. If you've been skipping periods (also a sign of pregnancy), you may need to see a gynecologist.

You Have Killer Cramps

Though cramping is normal when you get your period, you should see the doctor if your cramps are severe enough to interfere with normal activities, or if you get them even when it's not your time of the month.

You Have Problems Down There

We'll go more in depth in later chapters, but if you're experiencing any itching, burning, discoloration, odor, or other physical changes in the pubic or vaginal regions, you need to see a gynecologist right away.

Wellness Check-In: Seven Types of Medicine You Should Always Keep in Your Dorm Room

1. **Pain and fever medications:** Acetaminophen (such as Tylenol) and ibuprofen (Advil and Motrin).

2. **Antibiotic ointments:** These topical antibiotics can be applied to any cuts, burns, or open injuries to help prevent infection.

3. **Hydrocortisone:** A cortisone cream can relieve itching, such as from a bug bite or a rash. However, if the rash is serious, check with your doctor to make sure the cream won't make the condition worse.

4. **Antihistamines:** Keep both the drowsy and non-drowsy varieties on hand. These will help relieve the itching and watery nose/eyes symptoms you get from allergies.

5. **Decongestants:** These will help drain mucous from a stuffy nose.

6. **Cough medicines:** Keep both expectorants (which help your coughs become more productive by loosening mucous) and suppressants (which control your cough reflex) on hand.

Chapter Checklist

✓ You've heard it plenty of times, but we're going to drill it in one more time: Get. Plenty. Of. Sleep. That shuteye affects your mental and physical health, so getting enough of it is extremely important!

✓ If you're having a hard time falling asleep, make sure to take steps to help you catch those Zs—try putting your phone away an hour before bed or starting a bedtime ritual to help your body know when it's time to sleep.

✓ You're bound to catch something in college, but to avoid getting sick, make sure you're always disinfecting by washing your hands or using hand sanitizer. Also, even if you share *everything* with your bestie (secrets and all), you might not want to drink out of the same cup or use the same mascara.

✓ If you're sick, stay home! Most common illnesses found on college campuses can be treated with adequate rest (and lots of hydration). Plus, you'll want to avoid infecting your classmates.

✓ Be aware of the services your student health center offers, so you know where to go to seek medical care.

✓ Don't be afraid to see the doctor! You're in tune with your body, so if anything feels wrong, it very possibly could be.

✓ Be aware of seemingly minor symptoms you need to get checked out by a doctor, as they could be signs of a greater problem!

CHAPTER 7

Drinking, Smoking, and Drugs

"Work hard, play hard." It's a motto that many collegiettes take pretty seriously. After all, when you end up spending more hours in the library than all other activities combined, you need some way of letting loose! That's where the weekend comes in.

Your weekend debauchery may be well earned, but you shouldn't let all judgment fly out the window. Occasional bad behavior can turn into ongoing bad habits, and you might be surprised to learn just how serious even a small mistake can be. We're going to take a look at some of the most common substances on campus, how to know when you (or a friend) has taken it too far, and where you should go for help.

DRINKING

A couple of shots to pregame, a mixed drink or two at one party, a beer at the next—at least according to the movies, drinking in college seems like the norm. The question each weekend isn't *whether* you're going out (um, FOMO)—it's *where* you're going out, and more often than not, there's alcohol involved. Alcohol's prevalence in college culture means most people don't think twice about that extra shot . . . or two. But drinking in excess on a frequent basis could lead to alcohol poisoning, liver failure, or alcoholism, among other negative effects on your health. So how do you differentiate between normal college fun and risky behavior?

Common Risk Behaviors While Drinking

It's no surprise that alcohol impairs judgment (you had *how* many chicken nuggets last night?!), but it can have much more serious consequences than just thinking he's a ten when he's really a three thanks to beer goggles.

Blacking Out

"What *happened* last night?" Whether you've asked yourself that question after waking up on your bathroom floor or you've seen *The Hangover*, you know what blacking out is. Just how seriously should we take this alcohol-induced amnesia?

You may forget a portion of the night or wake up the next morning with no recollection of having gone out at all. Either way, blacking out can be scary, for a lot of reasons. You might wonder if you did anything to embarrass yourself—but this could be the least of your worries. While blacked out, you might have done something that put yourself or others at risk: driving under the influence, spending money with abandon, having unprotected sex, wandering off somewhere by yourself, or going home with a stranger.

So what are the best ways to avoid blacking out?

- Before you go out, set a limit for how many drinks you'll have.
- Pace yourself throughout the night—alternate alcoholic drinks with nonalcoholic drinks (water is best), and stick to the limit you set.

- Take each drink slowly. Sip, don't chug.
- Avoid shots and drinking games when possible, as both lead to a high level of alcohol consumption in a short period of time.
- Don't drink when you're sick or sleep-deprived, because you're likely to get drunk much more quickly.
- Don't mix alcohol with drugs or medications, which will intensify the effect of drinking (and could be life-threatening—more on that later).

And what should you do if you or a friend has blacked out? If it's during your night out and you notice that you or a friend is having trouble remembering something that happened an hour ago, be responsible and stop drinking. If possible, the best thing to do is to call it a night and head home. Otherwise, make a point to stay with your friends (or keep an eye on your friend) for the rest of the night.

If it's the morning after, get as many details about your night from your friends as you can. You need to know if you've done anything that requires medical attention or some sort of follow-up—for example, taking Plan B and visiting your doctor if you may have had unprotected sex.

How to Avoid a Terrible Hangover (and Deal with It If You Already Have One)

Eat before you drink—especially fats and carbs (hello, French fries). Stay hydrated throughout the night by alternating every drink with a glass of water, and drink slowly while you're at it. And don't take acetaminophen after you've been drinking—it's a dangerous combination. Instead, take ibuprofen.

Drunk Driving

Data published in the August 2010 issue of *Alcoholism: Clinical and Experimental Research* shows that one in five college students admitted driving drunk at some point, with 40 percent of students saying that they've been a passenger in a car with a drunk driver.

Knowing this statistic probably doesn't make you feel so good when you're headed to a bar with your friends on a Saturday night. So think twice before you get behind the wheel next time you've been drinking, even if you've only had two drinks, or if it's been hours since you had your last shot. Driving under the influence puts you and everybody around you at risk. If you don't have a designated driver for the night, call a cab—services like Uber and Lyft make it so easy to get cars instantly. Many colleges or surrounding communities also have resources where sober drivers will take you home for free, sometimes even in your own car so you won't have to head back to the bar the morning after to pick it up.

Mixing Alcohol with Other Substances

Taking medications with alcohol isn't just dangerous—it can be fatal. Here are the medications you should *definitely* avoid when drinking:

- Drugs with acetaminophen: Tylenol, Vicodin, Percocet
- Blood thinners
- Anti-seizure medications
- Antibiotics
- Antidepressants
- Adderall
- Pain medications (including OxyContin)
- Tetracycline
- Sudafed
- Cough syrup

Keep in mind that many manufacturers don't test their products with alcohol, so the list of drugs that react poorly to alcohol isn't comprehensive—your best bet is to avoid drinking after you've taken any medicine, period.

What happens when you mix alcohol with medication? It depends on the substance, but it could be anything from a nasty hangover to a blackout (after only a few drinks), vomiting, liver failure, difficulty breathing, or worse.

There *are* some medications that can be taken safely with alcohol when needed and in the correct dosage, but the stomach and intestinal lining can still be damaged by these combinations. Anti-inflammatory medications, such as ibuprofen (Advil, Motrin, etc.) or naproxen (Aleve, Naprosyn, etc.) are safe to mix with alcohol; you might take them to relieve hangover symptoms, for example. Your birth control pill won't have a negative reaction when taken with alcohol either, and it won't become less effective if you drink.

Unprotected Sex

You've had a few drinks and are having the best night ever. You've hit it off with a new guy and the two of you are tearing it up on the dance floor. A few hours and another shot later, he suggests heading back to his place.

Most of the time, a college hook-up ends up just being the subject of gossip among your friends or possibly in a bit of drama, but doing it with someone when your judgment is a little hazy can have real consequences. Whether he's a complete stranger, an acquaintance, or someone you know well, going home with a guy when you're wasted could put your safety and health at risk. You might be in the moment and forget to grab a condom, or consent (yours or his) might not be totally clear when you're both drunk— or worse, you might be putting yourself in the hands of somebody whose intentions go beyond just a hook-up. There's nothing wrong with a casual one-night stand, but know how to do it safely. Avoid going home drunk with a complete stranger; if you're not spending the night in your dorm room, make sure your friends know where you are; no matter what, use protection; and don't be afraid to speak up if the hook-up is going farther than what you're comfortable with (see Chapter 3 for more information).

Alcoholism

You might be thinking, "I'm not drinking enough to be an alcoholic—this doesn't apply to me." However, the early stages of alcoholism are often unrecognizable and hard to detect; generally, it starts when drinking becomes a habit, but not one that interferes with daily life. In the later stages of alcoholism, physical health deteriorates significantly and the individual is often in complete denial of the disorder. Those who start drinking between the ages of fifteen and twenty (as in, before or during college) have a one in ten chance of developing alcoholism later in life. Yikes.

Alcohol disorders generally stem from other emotional issues, so be mindful of how and why you're drinking. Are you chugging that jungle juice to get over a breakup? Is alcohol the only thing that can give you relief after a stressful week? If you're depending on alcohol at all as an emotional crutch, think again before reaching for the wine bottle. Even if you're not classified as an alcoholic now, using booze as an escape is setting yourself up to become an alcoholic years down the line. If you're concerned about your own or a friend's alcohol use, you'll find tons of local and national resources at the end of the chapter.

Avoiding Drinking in College

There are many reasons why collegiettes choose not to drink in college. The most important reason? Being underage. Though you'll have friends, roomies, and dormmates who may disagree and think underage drinking is not a big deal, there can be some pretty serious consequences if you're caught. In severe cases, you could be doing jail time; most likely you'll pay fines (not something you want to do on top of paying tuition!), do mandatory community service, or go to counseling, or you'll get your driver's license suspended. If you're caught using someone else's ID or a fake ID, the penalties vary by state—you could be slapped with a misdemeanor or even a felony. As for those who serve alcohol to minors? They could be charged with a crime, *especially* if someone is harmed as a result of drinking.

If you are of age, you still might choose to stay away from alcohol (even if you don't necessarily stay away from the social scene). Regardless of whether your reasons are based on personal or religious morals or health, don't let anybody try to put you down for your choices or pressure you into doing something you're not comfortable doing. If the people around you aren't supportive, you need to surround yourself with those who do respect your decisions. And if there are people who continue to give you a hard time no matter what, talk to your RA. Don't want to make a fuss about not drinking? Fill a Solo cup with water or soda when at a party, and no one needs to be the wiser.

SMOKING

The hazards that come with smoking are no secret by now. You already know that it can give you wrinkles and gum disease and will increase your chances of getting heart attacks and lung cancer. Given the (very serious) risk factors involved, why do many collegiettes continue to smoke?

"I'm a Social Smoker"

You've probably heard this one before—it's the collegiette who'll smoke once a week while out, or someone who only smokes when they drink. Sure, a few puffs every now and then isn't likely to raise the same health issues in you as it does in a chain-smoker, but each cigarette you smoke—even if it's not frequent—deteriorates your lungs, mouth, teeth, and heart to some extent. Plus, there's the very, very real possibility that you'll get addicted (it can happen after only one cigarette). One cigarette every Friday night easily transitions into three cigarettes a week, which then leads to a pack a day—all of a sudden, you *are* that chain-smoker.

"I Can Quit Anytime"

When it comes to worst-case scenarios, it's easy to think that it won't happen to you. You might think that you can enjoy a few cigarettes every now and then in college, but you'll quit before you have any long-term or life-threatening issues. You may tell yourself and the people around you that you have the willpower to quit any time you want. According to the American Cancer Society, however, that logic puts you in the minority: Only about four to seven percent of smokers actually succeed at quitting on their own; about twenty-five percent who use medications and/or therapy will be able to stop smoking for six months or more.

What Just One Cigarette Does to Your Body

Even just one cigarette can change your body. The first drag is the worst—you're inhaling a combination of the toxins from the lighter and what's in the cigarette. As you smoke, the levels of carbon monoxide in your lungs go up, making your heart work harder. Shortly after you inhale, nicotine hits the brain. The presence of nicotine results in increased heart rate and blood pressure, and slower circulation and constriction of blood vessels, causing everything from decreased skin temperature to tremors in your muscles. The smoke will reduce overall lung capacity and restrict airways, too, so you may find it harder to breathe.

The best way to beat smoking is to not start in the first place. But if you've already started smoking and are looking to quit, here are a few tips to get you started:

- **Nicotine patch:** Use one patch a day to slow cravings over a period of time.
- **Nicotine gum:** Chew a piece for a short period of time when you're experiencing sudden cravings.
- **Nicotine lozenges:** These work for sudden cravings as well.
- **Try a proven treatment (behavioral or pharmacological).** These can help increase your chances of staying smoke-free.
- And if you don't succeed right away? **Try again—and keep trying—until you do.** We've listed a series of resources and hotlines at the end of this chapter to help you through this!

DRUGS

College is known to be a time when it's okay to be a little experimental. You try a bunch of classes out before deciding on your major, or you become more open with your sexuality. For some, college also means a time to experiment with drugs. Depending on the substance, there is a certain level of risk involved when using drugs, some more severe than others. And legal or not, if there's something you're looking for, we can almost guarantee that *someone* on campus is going to be able to get it for you. With drugs being relatively easy to access at school, it's even more important that you know why you should stay away. We're going to go over what you might find on campus—and what the consequences of possessing or using these substances are.

Party Drugs

If there's one thing you're sure to find at almost every college party—aside from alcohol—it's marijuana, whether it's being smoked or taken as an edible (such as a weed brownie or cookie). And in certain states, not just its medical use but its recreational use is legal.

So it can't be that bad, right? Well, that depends. Marijuana works by stimulating your brain cells to release more dopamine, which explains why for most people, a weed high feels relaxing and even euphoric. But as collegiettes, your brains are still developing, so long-term use could result in interference with your brain functions. While overdosing and dying from taking too much marijuana is unlikely, an excessive amount can make you physically sick; you may also experience psychological effects, such as extreme paranoia or panic attacks. And studies have shown that driving high is just as dangerous as driving drunk, so don't even think about getting behind the wheel if you've been smoking (or about getting in the car of someone who's high).

Then there are the other party drugs—the ones made popular by the club and rave scenes of the '70s and '80s.

Though less prevalent than marijuana, other popular drugs you might find on campus include prescription painkillers, which can mimic the feeling of getting drunk (but act faster and are longer lasting); ecstasy and cocaine, which will increase your drive for intimacy (suddenly, everybody is your BFF), heighten your senses to light and sound, and keep your energy going all night; and LSD and shrooms, hallucinogens that can give you hours-long trips that alter your sense of time, space, and self.

Each of these drugs has its own set of risks, many of which could be (and have been) fatal. None of them mix well with alcohol, yet because they're usually taken while partying on weekends, they're often taken with drinks, increasing your risk of an overdose. Many of them are sold not in their pure form, but as drug cocktails (which may include hard drugs such as meth or heroin), so you don't *really* know what you're taking. Overdoses could result in consequences such as a failed liver, extreme dehydration, hallucinations, and enough paranoia to hurt yourself or others; and this is just the abridged version. Steer clear!

> ### Five Signs Your Partying Is a Problem
> **1.** You're sleep deprived or can't fall asleep.
> **2.** Your grades are slipping.
> **3.** Your mood is changing constantly, or is easily affected even by small things—you often feel anxious or depressed.
> **4.** You're having more conflicts with roommates, friends, and family.
> **5.** You're getting sick more often than usual.

Study Drugs

Exams, final projects, huge papers—the list of things you need to cram into your schedule seems to far exceed the amount of time you have. So you take a caffeine pill to keep you from nodding off at your desk at night, and bolster it with a coffee (venti, please) the next morning, after you've gotten no sleep. You might feel a little weird (especially when that caffeine wears off and you crash in the middle of your history lecture), but it's just temporary, so you think it's fine.

As it turns out, it's all too easy to abuse caffeine, and you've probably done it before—without even knowing it. Like any drug, caffeine *is* addictive, and when you don't get your daily dose, you can experience withdrawal symptoms such as headaches, fatigue, irritability, and insomnia. And when you have too much caffeine (as in, more than 300 mg—that's about three cups of coffee, otherwise known as a standard day in a collegiette's life), you can experience caffeine intoxication, which includes symptoms like dehydration, anxiety, an irregular or rapid heart rate, and disorientation. And that's just in the short term. Long-term use could result in serious medical issues, such as stomach ulcers, acid reflux, breast cysts, sleep disorders, depression, and delusions or psychosis. Put that umpteenth cup of coffee down. Yep, that's what we thought.

Caffeine's not the only stimulant college students use regularly to keep themselves in the game. Prescription drugs like Adderall and Ritalin, used to treat attention deficit disorders (ADD and ADHD), are used to maintain a higher level of energy and an increased ability to focus. When you're halfway through midterms, these drugs might seem like magic pills that keep you working productively—it's a miracle, you actually *want* to get through that stats textbook! But without a prescription, these drugs aren't only illegal, they can also be dangerous for your health.

Taken without a doctor's supervision (under which you'd be given the correct dosage based on your needs), these stimulants can result in extreme crashes once the drug wears off, leaving you feeling fatigued and depressed. You may also experience increased blood pressure and heart rate, nervousness, and insomnia—even after using the drug just once. Symptoms of overdose include aggressive behavior, uncontrollable shaking, dizziness, vomiting, and hallucinations.

WHAT TO DO WHEN DRINKING, SMOKING, OR DRUG USE BECOMES A PROBLEM

How can you tell the difference between the use versus the abuse of drugs and alcohol? There are several physical, behavioral, and mental symptoms to look out for that can be signs of abuse:

Physical
- Bloodshot eyes, or unusual pupil size
- Excessive weight loss or weight gain
- Lack of coordination or stability
- Shakes, tremors, and seizures (in someone without a family medical history of these conditions)
- Poor physical appearance and hygiene

- Slurred speech
- Unexplained injuries
- Unusual smells on breath

Behavioral
- Poor performance at school or at work
- Loss of motivation; lack of interest in activities formerly enjoyed
- Unusually frequent need for money, or unexplained financial problems—may lead to borrowing or stealing money
- Unexplained change in relationships with family and friends
- Withdrawal

Psychological
- Changes in personality
- Susceptibility to mood swings; will laugh or become angry easily even when inappropriate
- Anxiety or paranoia
- Lethargy

As always, if you feel that you or someone you know may be in immediate physical danger because of her drinking or drug abuse, call 911 or go to the emergency room right away. If you recognize any of these symptoms in a friend, don't be afraid to confront her about them, making sure to let her know your concern comes from a good place. Chances are she'll be in denial—if the behavior continues and/or worsens, get in touch with a family member or someone close to her.

WHERE TO FIND DRUG- AND ALCOHOL-RELATED RESOURCES

If you or a friend is struggling with drugs or alcohol, there are many resources available to you.

Medical and Counseling Services on Campus

Most colleges have resources that will grant you amnesty and work with you through your drug and alcohol problems, no questions asked. Start with your student health and counseling centers, who'll be able to help you directly or point you to the right on-campus resources. If you go to a school with a strict set of values where infractions result in penalties, or that has a no-tolerance policy, try the following local off-campus resources in your community.

The National Council on Alcoholism and Drug Dependence (*www.ncadd.org*)

This site has a "Find an Affiliate" tool that allows you to search local groups and organizations that are carefully vetted by the NCADD. They all specialize in the treatment of drug and alcohol abuse and addiction, and aim to prevent, educate, and help in the recovery process. You'll also find resources and support groups geared specifically for the family and friends of those dealing with drug or alcohol abuse.

American Society of Addiction Medicine (*www.asam.org*)

If you are battling addiction specifically, the ASAM's site has a search function that will bring up the doctors in your area who specialize in addiction; having a doctor who is trained and certified in drug and alcohol addiction can make a huge difference in your recovery.

Alcoholics Anonymous (*www.aa.org*)

Looking for a support group rather than medical aid? AA is open to anybody who has a drinking problem at any age, even if you don't qualify as an alcoholic. There are locations not only across the country but also worldwide; a quick search on the website will tell you where the nearest meeting is.

Recovery.org (*www.recovery.org*)

Not only will you be able to find great information for your own recovery on this site, but you can also get in touch with an interventionist, who will create a program to help someone who is in denial about his or her drug- or alcohol-related issues.

Rehabs.com (*www.rehabs.com*)

If you feel that you or a friend has reached the point where it's necessary to stay in a rehab facility, start your search here. You can search by location or type of rehab (even down to the specific substance), and the site will connect you with the center that's the best fit for you.

Centers for Disease Control and Prevention (*www.cdc.gov*)

The CDC has a great campaign, Tips From Former Smokers, where you can read inspiring stories from people from all walks of life who have successfully quit smoking. It'll help you see that not only are you not alone, but that it's possible to quit, too.

Smoke Free Women (*http://women.smokefree.gov*)

Geared specifically towards women, this site offers tools, tips, and other information about quitting smoking. There's a focus on women's health issues, with sections of the site also dedicated to your overall health, both mental and physical. You can even access a whole network of women who are quitting or have quit smoking to help you get through the process.

Freedom From Smoking Online (*www.ffsonline.org*)

A part of the American Lung Association, this site is dedicated to helping you quit smoking, no matter where you are. The site offers a series of online courses that walk you through the steps to quitting, and is great if your schedule is busy or isn't very flexible, since everything is done online, any time of the day.

National Hotlines

You can also call several helplines either to speak with someone right away, or just to get some more guided information on what the best course of action is for you or a friend:

- SAMHSA National Helpline/Treatment Referral Routing Service: 1-800-662-HELP (1-800-662-4357) (*www.samhsa.gov/find-help/national-helpline*)
- *Recovery.com*'s Addiction Treatment: 1-888-737-4105
- The Alcohol & Drug Addiction Resource Center: 1-800-390-4056
- National Cocaine Hotline: 1-800-COCAINE (1-800-262-2463)
- Alcohol Abuse and Crisis Intervention: 1-800-234-0246
- National Cancer Institute (Smoking): 1-877-44U-QUIT (1-877-448-7848)
- Tobacco Quitline: 1-800-QUIT-NOW (1-800-784-8669)

Wellness Check-In: Five Rules for Safe Drinking

1. Don't drink on an empty stomach.
2. Never leave your drink unattended. You never know when someone could slip something into your drink.
3. Hydrate, hydrate, hydrate! Alternate alcoholic drinks with water throughout the night.
4. Set your drink limit before the night begins and stick to it.
5. Always have a sober designated driver or arrange for transportation so neither you nor your friends will be tempted to get behind the wheel (even if you think you're okay to drive).

Chapter Checklist

✓ No blackout should be taken lightly. If it happens to you or a friend, get together and recount the night; if you've engaged in any risky behavior, such as having unprotected sex, you'll need to follow up appropriately.

✓ Avoid mixing drugs and alcohol. If you have taken or you need to take medicine on a night you're planning on drinking, make sure it's not something that has a risk of a negative reaction. If you're not sure, it's best to avoid it entirely.

✓ Know the signs of alcohol poisoning or a drug overdose, and if it happens to you or a friend, go to the emergency room right away. It could be a matter of life or death, and it can't wait. Be honest with the doctors about what you or your friend used over the course of the night so they can start the appropriate treatment; they likely won't involve law enforcement, even when it comes to the use of illegal substances.

✓ Smoking is addictive, period, and with every cigarette comes the decline of your health (and arguably the health of those around you).

✓ Study drugs—including caffeine!—are drugs, too; they can be addictive and harmful to your health.

✓ Know the difference between using drugs and alcohol and abusing drugs and alcohol by looking for signs of abuse—and where to go for help.

CHAPTER 8

Mental Health

Maybe it's your freshman year and you're just learning how to juggle classes and your social life all while being far from home for the first time. Or maybe you're an upperclassman who's just added an internship to her already busy schedule and is dealing with relationship trouble at the same time. At some point during your four years of college, you'll be faced with changes to your schedule, life, and more—all of which may take a toll on your well-being. It's important to understand the factors that can affect your mental health, how to deal with them, and how to know when to seek help—for yourself or for a friend.

STRESS

"The best four years of my life." There's probably about a 97 percent chance that someone said these words to you before you left for college.

College has a pretty glorified reputation, especially in the minds of those who haven't written a paper or taken an economics exam in a couple of decades. But let's be real: College isn't all toga parties and sunbathing in the quad. You're living away from home for the first time, managing a packed schedule, and trying to maintain a solid GPA as well as an enviable social life. You might even sometimes try to get some sleep! The bottom line: While college can afford you loads of incredible experiences, it can also be a stressful place.

The Different Kinds of Stress

Believe it or not, stress can be a good thing! Known as eustress, this good form of stress can motivate you to push yourself (without getting overwhelmed). It can help you stay focused and on top of things, and it challenges you in a positive way to achieve your goals.

Then there's acute stress, which, as a collegiette, you'll likely deal with from time to time throughout college and beyond. You'll experience acute stress when big changes or events come up: a tight deadline, a breakup, a final exam in a subject that's not your forte, etc.

Lastly, there's chronic stress, which is an ongoing form of stress that wears on you day by day. In the case of chronic stress, stress becomes a constant. If you don't do anything to relieve it, chronic stress can lead to serious mental and physical consequences.

How to Know When You're Too Stressed

It's important to recognize that each person has a different tolerance for certain stressors. Just because your roommate can take on an extra few volunteer hours a week without feeling overworked doesn't mean you should be able to as well, or just because your best friend is adding credits to her schedule isn't reason enough for you to be doing it, too.

So think about this: What do you have to do today?

Does your stomach twist into knots in response to this question? Are you feeling overwhelmed by a long list of claims on your time? Do you ever feel that you're spreading yourself too thin, even though you're a willing participant in everything that's eating up your time?

If any of this sounds familiar, it may be time to reevaluate what you're doing and cut down on the areas that are causing you stress. Consider which type of stress you're experiencing. Your stress levels are most likely manageable if they only spike when finals season begins. But if they're rising constantly in reaction to both big and small events, you'll need to make some changes.

Relieving Stress

Try one of these strategies for nipping stress in the bud.

Make a List

A lot of stress in college can come from feeling as if your life is chaotic or disorganized. If this sounds like you, make a list so you can see all your responsibilities in one place, which will allow you to prioritize. Plus, it's much more difficult to justify procrastinating with that extra Netflix episode when you can clearly see everything you need to get done. While some people prefer the good old-fashioned pen-and-paper list, there are also plenty of list apps you can download on your smartphone, so play around with different methods and figure out what works best for you.

Maintain a Healthy Lifestyle

The thought of scheduling gym time into an already packed schedule may seem daunting, but it's more than worth it. Not only will exercise improve your physical health, but exercising also releases endorphins, which help reduce stress.

Rather than just hitting the gym whenever you feel you have time (which may be never!), set aside regular times each week to work out. See if you can make plans with a friend to go with you, or find a class at your school's gym that you'll feel excited to attend each week (Beyoncé yoga? Yes, please!).

Meditate

Taking a few minutes out of each day to meditate and give your mind a break can do wonders for your mental health.

When and where you like to meditate is up to you. You might prefer to meditate in the morning, when your mind is most at ease. Or you might want to try meditating as a study break to reset before diving back into your American Lit reading. Or you could opt for an end-of-day meditation, to clear your mind of the day's activities and set yourself up for more peaceful sleep.

However you find time for meditation, there are a few key aspects to making it effective:

- **Set your posture.** Though meditation is about relaxation, your posture should be kept alert. Keep your back straight, even sitting against a wall if it helps, and let your muscles hang freely, with your hands resting on your knees or lap. Close your eyes and draw your attention inward.
- **Find your focus.** Tune in to your breath as it enters and leaves your nostrils. You can also direct your attention to the rise and fall of your chest, or other sensations that occur in your body as you breathe. Whatever you choose to focus on, stay with that object for at least ten breaths.
- **Relax deeply.** Starting with the top of your scalp, move down through your body slowly as you soften your muscles. You might be surprised at how many places you're holding tension!

Start with meditating for a few minutes at a time; as you get used to the practice, you can increase the time you spend meditating and find what works best for you. Meditating strengthens your mind, gives you better concentration, allows you to think more clearly, and calms your nerves in times of increased stress, among other benefits.

Looking for more ideas like these? You'll find more tips on time management and dealing with an overpacked schedule in Chapter 16.

Make Sleep a Priority

We know it's easier said than done, but getting eight hours of sleep every night should be a priority! There will inevitably be days where you're up all night putting finishing touches on a big research paper, but late nights should not be the norm. Help yourself fall asleep and stay asleep by turning your electronic devices off an hour before bed (that Instagram like can wait until tomorrow morning), not using your bed as a space for homework (so you condition your body to recognize it as a place for rest and recuperation), and actually getting up when your alarm rings in the morning so you're tired enough the following evening to get to bed at a decent hour.

ANXIETY

Letting your stress continue to build without taking steps to reduce it or seeking professional help can lead to more than just a couple of bad days or weeks. One possible outcome is anxiety. According to the National Institute of Mental Health, anxiety disorders affect approximately 18 percent of adults ages eighteen and up, meaning it's not uncommon among college-aged women.

The trick is in knowing where to draw the line between everyday anxiety and a disorder. As with your levels of stress, it's normal to experience anxiety on a limited basis—when you're stressing over a huge exam, for example, it's natural (and even healthy) to feel a little anxious.

But if the anxiety is continual, is something you feel is out of your control, and is affecting your day-to-day life (you're missing classes, your grades are slipping, you're pulling away from friendships and other relationships), it's time to do something about it. See our list of resources that can be of help towards the end of this chapter.

What You Can Do about Anxiety

If your anxiety isn't debilitating, it's possible you could manage it on your own. If your anxiety comes as a result of factors such as exams, for example, you probably feel impending doom as midterms or finals approach (and not just the normal pre-test jitters). Perhaps your mind blanks as soon as you sit down and pick your pencil up, or, in some cases, you might even have a panic attack. Fortunately, there are ways to cope with these situational bouts of anxiety:

- **Get enough sleep.** Avoid pulling all-nighters, which will leave you fatigued and more likely to grab that extra coffee in the morning—caffeine can heighten the effects of anxiety! Aim for at least eight hours of shut-eye each night.
- **Plan ahead.** Anxiety over exams can be triggered by a sense of unpreparedness, so if you schedule study time throughout the week before your test, you'll feel ready to tackle that final ahead of time.
- **Stay calm the day of the test.** Before you get out of bed that morning, take a couple of deep breaths—and do the same when you get to class. When anxiety triggers a panic attack, breathing becomes quick and shallow, so controlling it will set a more relaxed mood right away.
- **Treat yourself after the test!** This gives you the opportunity to congratulate yourself for getting through the exam—and hopefully acing it!

DEPRESSION

Another mental health issue that can strike in college is depression.

What Are the Symptoms of Depression?

If you are depressed, you might:

- Feel sad—all the time
- Stop enjoying activities you used to love
- Have a sense of hopelessness

- Experience changes in your sleep schedule, appetite, and personal hygiene
- Have a hard time concentrating
- Become irritable
- Withdraw from friends and family (social isolation)
- Drink or use drugs uncharacteristically
- Have a hard time finding positive thoughts
- Have thoughts of suicide and death

The number and severity of symptoms can vary between individuals—some might be able to check off this entire list, while others might only exhibit one or two of these symptoms. And the disorder can manifest itself in different ways—some people become agitated and restless, while others become vegetative and withdrawn.

So how do you know if you are actually depressed or if you've just got the (non-clinical) blues?

Only a professional will be able to diagnose depression. It's very hard to determine yourself if you are depressed. Unfortunately, this also means that it's common for depression to go unnoticed, as you may shrug it off as having a bad couple of weeks. If your sadness is unusually prolonged, or if you're having any thoughts of self-harm or suicide, it's absolutely vital that you visit your student health center or reach out through one of the other resources mentioned towards the end of this chapter to get the help you need.

HOMESICKNESS

No matter how many new friends you make at college or how much fun you have, sometimes the only place you want to be is home.

Homesickness happens when you miss what's familiar, such as the support system your family and friends at home provide and the places and things you love. If you're a freshman, it's not unusual to feel overwhelmed by all of the changes. But even once you're beyond freshman year, you may still miss home in a very real way from time to time.

Ways to Overcome Homesickness

- **Explore campus and the new city you're in.** Take a friend so you make memories with those around you, too!
- **Join a club.** You'll meet people who have similar interests and spend time doing what you love.
- **Stay in touch with family and friends back home.** Skype, Google Chat, text, FaceTime—update your family and friends on your new life so they feel like a part of it, too. Just be sure this isn't replacing time you could be using to forge new relationships.
- **Plan a trip back home.** Whether it's a weekend or for the holidays, booking your flight and creating an itinerary gives you something to look forward to.
- **Talk about how you feel.** Especially during your first year at school, it's likely that many of your peers are experiencing the same feelings. Knowing you're not in it alone can help you cope!

WHAT TO DO WHEN YOUR FRIEND IS GOING THROUGH A TOUGH TIME

Just as you should know when to ask for help for yourself, you should also know when to step in and offer help for someone else. But when a friend is going through a difficult time, it's hard to know what you should do to help. Are you doing too little, or are you overstepping boundaries? Whether she's dealing with the loss of a loved one, a medical situation, family problems, a breakup, or anything else causing her distress, it hurts to see that someone you care about is hurting. If you find yourself in this situation, here's what you need to know.

Accept That You Cannot Fix Everything

As much as you want to help, you have to recognize that many things are out of your control. Sometimes you don't have the means to help or even the best advice to offer. Do the best that you can to help your friend in whatever situation she is in, even if it means just offering your support by listening and giving her only what she asks for.

Let Her Know That You Will Be There for Her

Take cues from your friend to gauge what it is she needs, whether she needs someone to speak with or needs you to give her space. Respect her decision either way, but remind her that you will be there for her, no matter what—and stick to that promise. Taking on the emotional burden of a friend in need can be taxing on you as well, and showing her you're available doesn't mean picking and choosing when you can help, so don't back out when it gets tough. Still not sure what you can do? Think about ways you can make her day easier—run errands for her, offer to return her library books, or even just send her a card expressing your sympathy.

Listen Without Judging Her

Everybody has opinions, but even if the advice you offer comes from a good place, it might not be what your friend needs to hear. Focus on lending your ear, because even if a friend asks for your advice, what she may really be looking for is to get her feelings off her chest. That's why it's more important to listen than to speak. Beware of dominating the conversation with stories about your own life. Even though these stories might be brought up with the intention of relating to your friend, be careful not to make the conversation about you. Focus on your friend and what she's going through.

Don't Downplay the Situation

It might seem helpful to encourage your friend to look on the bright side, but doing this might not help at all. Avoid saying things like "You still have a lot to be thankful for" or "It could be worse." Comments like these could make her feel that her feelings aren't valid. Instead, remind her that she's human and she's allowed to feel whatever she is feeling.

Don't Treat Her Too Differently

There is a time and a place to sit and let her cry on your shoulder, but that time is not every second of every day. When she needs to have a conversation about what's going on in her life, be there for her—but during the rest of the day, don't feel that you need to walk on eggshells or treat her like she's fragile. Doing so will only emphasize her situation, even during times when she just wants to feel normal. Be sure to remind her that she's not a burden on you, however—acting *too* normal may make her feel you'd rather pretend like nothing's wrong than deal with any problems that may exist, so make sure she knows you want to help in any way you can.

What Happens If She Refuses Your Help When She Needs It?

In some situations, a friend might refuse your help (for example, in the case of an addiction that she denies). Don't perceive this response as her pushing you away because she doesn't really need the help—if she's in denial or is clearly suffering, it may be even more important that you step in.

Often, the idea of getting help may be overwhelming for your friend. If she's depressed, for instance, gathering the energy to search for mental health professionals (and then find the right fit for her) can be difficult or impossible. If this is the case, be proactive and take it upon yourself to put a list of resources together for your friend. You can even take it to the next step and call the therapists and psychiatrists on your list to see if they're accepting new patients—encouraging her to take the first step may be more successful if you've made that step easier for her to take.

If it's a case where your friend's situation may be life-threatening to herself or others, you need to contact the campus health center or a crisis hotline. If it's an immediate emergency, call 911.

WHERE TO FIND HELP ON CAMPUS AND OFF

When you think of your college campus, you generally consider it a place to learn—it's where you take your classes, spend time studying, and go to club meetings. It's more than just school, though. College is full of resources no matter what your needs are, from rare books for your research project to, yes, mental health and counseling (and so, so much more).

Often, collegiettes may hesitate to seek help, whether they know they need it or not. Unfortunately, there's often a negative stigma surrounding mental illness. Like many young women, you might feel embarrassed that you need somebody else's help to deal with problems in your life, or see yourself as inadequate when you come to a point where you do need help. But when faced with difficulty, especially if it's interfering with your life, you need to set those misconceptions aside, because your health must come first.

Your Campus Health or Counseling Center

Many universities across the country offer their students free therapy, so even if you think your case is mild, it can only benefit you to set up an appointment. If free individual counseling isn't available, other schools have free group sessions, or will at least do a free initial visit to help you determine what you need to start your path to recovery. At the very least, your campus health center will be able to refer you to places where you can get help, and should be willing to work within your budget, schedule, and other needs.

Some schools also have mental health centers or resources that cater specifically to women and women's issues, so check to see if there's a similar resource at your school.

Your Campus Helpline

Of course, there are national hotlines you can call any time of the day, but sometimes what you need is to speak to a peer or someone in a similar environment who might better understand the things that are going on in a collegiette's life. Many schools have peer-run hotlines where you can call in anonymously and speak to a trained individual your own age. They'll also be able to provide you with places you can go on campus for more help, if that's what you're looking for.

Mental Health Awareness Clubs and Organizations

Even if your college doesn't have a peer counseling service, you may find that there are on-campus student organizations you can reach out to. They may not be licensed to diagnose or treat mental illness, but they will definitely know what resources are available on campus as well as in the surrounding area, and they may be able to help connect you.

Your RA

RAs have received at least basic training for dealing with mental health issues. They have your best interests at heart, and if you've formed a great mentorship bond with your RA, it may be easier for you to confide in him or her first rather than your roommates, your friends, or even your family, and your RA can point you in the right direction for more help.

ULifeline

No matter where in the country you are, ULifeline (*www.ulifeline*
.org) will connect you with mental health resources in your area. A
quick search for your school will bring up any counseling centers or
emergency contact numbers on campus. The site also offers information
on a variety of common issues students deal with (alcohol and drugs,
anxiety, eating disorders, depression, and more), a self-evaluation to
help you determine the kind of help you need, and a comprehensive
list of national twenty-four-hour hotlines you can call anytime.

National Hotlines

There are a number of national-based resources that you can
seek anytime, anywhere:

- National Suicide Prevention Lifeline: 1-800-273-TALK
  (1-800-273-8255) (*www.suicidepreventionlifeline.org*)
- The Trevor Lifeline (Suicide Prevention for LGBTQ+ Youth):
  866-4-U-TREVOR (1-866-488-7386) (*www.thetrevorproject
  .org*)
- Mental Health America: 800-969-NMHA (1-800-969-6642)
  (*www.mentalhealthamerica.net*)
- SAMHSA National Helpline/Treatment Referral Routing
  Service: 1-800-662-HELP (1-800-662-4357) (*www.samhsa
  .gov/find-help/national-helpline*)
- National Sexual Assault Hotline: 1-800-656-HOPE (1-800-656-
  4673) (*www.rainn.org/get-help/national-sexual-assault-hotline*)
- National Teen Dating Abuse Helpline: 1-866-331-9474
  (*www.loveisrespect.org*)
- National Domestic Violence Hotline: 1-800-799-SAFE
  (1-800-799-7233) (*www.thehotline.org*)
- National Association of Anorexia Nervosa and Associated
  Disorders: 630-577-1330 (*www.anad.org*)

- National Eating Disorders Association Information and Referral Helpline: 1-800-931-2237 (*www.nationaleatingdisorders.org*)

Wellness Check-In: Nine Signs You or a Friend Needs Mental Health Help

1. You've been feeling down for a prolonged period of time.
2. You either go out and pack your schedule with new activities (in an effort to take your mind off of what's going on) or start to withdraw from everything you're doing.
3. Your sleep patterns and/or appetite change drastically.
4. You have thoughts about suicide, whether or not you have plans to take action.
5. Your grades are falling.
6. Anything that doesn't fall within your regular routine causes you stress and anxiety.
7. You are experiencing regular panic attacks.
8. You start using—or relying on—alcohol and/or drugs.
9. You stop taking care of yourself and your personal hygiene.

Chapter Checklist

✓ Learn to recognize the difference between a stressful or bad day versus chronic stress, clinical anxiety, and depression. Being reasonably stressed, fatigued, or even sad (such as when you're in the middle of finals week or feeling a little homesick) is totally normal, but when these feelings are triggered by small events or even nothing at all (and you're feeling down *all* the time), you may need to take action and find help.

✓ Taking care of your physical health with proper diet, nutrition, and exercise can make a huge difference in your mental health, too.

✓ Don't be afraid to reach out to others when you need their support—this includes everyone from family and friends to leaders and administrators on campus.

✓ Know how to talk to a friend who is going through a hard time, whether temporary or long-term. The most important thing is to let her know you're there for her, no matter what!

✓ Know where to go for help, on campus and off. Your college has tons of resources (like a health center, student organizations, and free therapy and counseling) that can provide you with everything you need to get back on track. There are also several national hotlines and organizations that specialize in mental health–related issues that can either help you directly or refer you to resources in your community.

CHAPTER 9

Sexual Health

By the time you get to college, you should be going to the doctor for more than just the occasional flu. It's recommended that you start seeing a gynecologist between ages thirteen to fifteen (though a pelvic exam likely won't be necessary at this age), and by twenty-one, you should be getting yearly Pap smears. Regardless of your age, you should definitely see your gynecologist if you plan on being sexually active or if you're already sexually active.

Whether it's your first time visiting your gynecologist or you're headed back for your annual visit, the thought of the exam can be a little nerve-racking. When selecting a gynecologist, make sure it's somebody you're comfortable with and can trust, even if you think your preferences might be nitpicky (for example, if you prefer a female doctor, or if you feel more comfortable speaking about women's health issues with a younger doctor).

WHAT SHOULD YOU EXPECT DURING A VISIT TO YOUR GYNECOLOGIST?

When you first head in, you'll meet with your doctor to chat about your overall health—at this point you'll go over your personal and family medical history, any health concerns you may have (such as unusual discharge, any discomfort, itching or burning, etc.), as well as your sexual history. Be *completely* honest with your doctor!

For the exam, you'll be asked to remove all your clothes (including your bra and underpants). You'll put on a disposable hospital gown and lie down on the table. The doctor will then feel your neck and examine your breasts, the area under your arms, your stomach, and the area around your bikini line. He or she is feeling for any abnormalities or tenderness that could indicate diseases such as breast cancer.

The pelvic exam comes next. This part is what generally makes collegiettes most nervous, but take a few deep breaths to relax. As part of the exam, the doctor will use a cotton swab to take a sample of your cervical fluids, which will be used for your Pap smear (tests for cervical cancer) and to test for the human papillomavirus.

Unless you experience any unusual symptoms, such as itching, redness, burning or other pain, unusual discharge, or irregular bleeding, you'll only have to see your gynecologist once a year! Don't let the discomfort of the exam stop you from going. You wouldn't ignore pain in your stomach or a rash on your body, so view your sexual health as something to be just as vigilant about.

WOMEN'S HEALTH ISSUES YOU SHOULD BE AWARE OF

We've been over the symptoms that indicate a visit to the gynecologist is in order, but what exactly do those symptoms mean? Whether you're sexually active or not, there are a number of health issues you should know about that can affect women. Here are some of the most common ones:

Urinary Tract Infection (UTI)

A UTI will cause a burning sensation when you urinate, or make you feel as if you have to pee all the time (even when you don't). It occurs when bacteria enters the urinary tract; sexual intercourse is one way this can happen. You'll need a prescription for antibiotics to treat the infection.

Human Papillomavirus (HPV)

Most people who have HPV may never know they've been infected; in the majority of cases, an infected person sees no symptoms before his or her immune system beats the virus (which can take two years). In more severe cases, it can cause genital warts, or even cervical cancer. It's a sexually transmitted infection, and since there is no real treatment, it's highly recommended that young men and women be vaccinated against it.

Yeast Infection

Most women will experience a yeast infection in their lifetimes—it's that common. Though it can be spread through intercourse, it's not exclusively a sexually transmitted infection. It'll cause itching and burning, as well as thicker, white discharge. You can generally treat yeast infections with over-the-counter vaginal creams, but if they're ineffective, see your doctor for a prescription. A doctor can also confirm that what you have is a yeast infection as opposed to a bacterial one.

Polycystic Ovary Syndrome (PCOS)

An endocrine disorder caused by a hormonal imbalance, PCOS results in cysts in your ovaries, irregular periods, excessive hair growth, and acne. It is usually prevalent in women who are overweight. Treatment will depend on your condition and what your major symptoms are; your doctor may recommend a low-calorie diet for weight loss, or put you on birth control medication to make your periods more regular and/or help control the excessive hair growth.

Breast Cancer

Breast cancer, which forms in breast tissue, is best detected through a mammogram. If your gynecologist discovers any unusual lumps (or if you find them through your own self-exams), getting a mammogram might be the next step. How it's treated will depend on your individual situation, but fortunately, breast cancer is very treatable when detected in the early stages.

Serious Conditions That Bad Cramps Could Be a Sign Of

Having cramps during your period isn't anything to be concerned about—when they're normal. But if they're abnormally severe (enough to make you double over and have to stay home), you'll want to pay your gynecologist a visit—you could have one of these three conditions.

Pelvic Inflammatory Disease (PID)

An infection of the uterine lining, which can spread to your fallopian tubes, PID can be a complication of some STDs. When should you see your doctor? Usually, cramps are at their worst in the morning, and throughout the day they improve. With PID, it's the opposite—so schedule an appointment if your cramps get worse as the day goes on.

Ovarian Torsion

This happens when an ovary rotates out of its proper place, and usually occurs when you have ovarian cysts. You'll know the cramps aren't normal if the pain is localized (usually on one side of your body).

Ectopic Pregnancy

Pregnancies usually develop in the uterus, but in a case where it does occur outside of the womb (typically in the fallopian tubes), you'll experience cramps so severe that you won't mistake them for regular ones. They also usually occur on one side of the body, and you may experience typical pregnancy symptoms, such as tender breasts or nausea.

Keep Notes on Your Reproductive Health

Nothing's more annoying than going to your doctor because of a medical problem and realizing you don't know the answers to some of the basic questions she's asking you, such as the date of your last period or on what days of your cycle your cramps are most severe. For your own preparedness as well as in case of any medical issues, make a habit of noting the first and last day of your period each month (try jotting it in a tiny notebook you keep in your nightstand), as well as anything noteworthy about how you felt during your period. This will help you predict when your next period will arrive so you can have the necessary supplies on hand, not to mention it's useful info to have if anything necessitates a visit to the doctor's office.

EVERYTHING YOU NEED TO KNOW ABOUT HAVING SAFE SEX

No matter whether you're hooking up with multiple people or you're having sex with a long-term boyfriend, it's important to have safe sex. And we don't just mean preventing pregnancy—there's a lot more to be mindful of when it comes to having safe sex. From birth control to STDs, we're going to prep you with everything you need to know before taking it to the bedroom.

The Beginner's Guide to the Pill (and Other Contraceptives)

So, you want to start taking birth control. With all the options available, where do you even begin? You'll find that many college women are on "the pill" (and there is more than one kind), but you can also consider other methods such as an intrauterine device

(IUD), vaginal ring, or the patch. You need to discuss which option works best for you with your doctor or gynecologist, but we'll review the basics so you can go into that conversation informed.

The Pill

There are several varieties of birth control pills alone—the most common is a combination pill, which contains both estrogen and progestin. You'll take a pill a day for a twenty-one- or twenty-eight-day period, with placebo pills in between (you'll get your period during the placebo week). If taken correctly (as in, at the same time each day), these pills are 99 percent effective at preventing pregnancy.

Then there's the progestin-only pill, which is a safer option for anybody who has or is at risk for heart disease or blood clots (this includes smokers). In order to be effective, it needs to be taken at the same exact time every day—you may be okay within a three-hour window, but use backup and/or emergency contraception if you're later than that.

You can also get extended cycle pills, which you can take continuously for three months up to a whole year at a time without any placebos—which means you won't get your period every month. Some may rejoice at never having to deal with their time of month, but many collegiettes prefer to get their period every month (if for nothing but confirmation that they're not pregnant!).

For the most part, there aren't huge risks to taking the pill, but that depends solely on your personal and family health history, so be sure you know those details before discussing options with your doctor. Once you start birth control, warning signs to watch out for include migraines, blurred vision, leg pain, chest pain, and abdominal pain; these can all indicate a possible stroke or heart attack as a result of blood clots. One reason you'll know that the pill isn't right for you: if you can't remember to take it at the same time every day. It's not effective unless used correctly, so look into other options if you know you'll have a hard time remembering.

The Patch

The patch is a small adhesive-bandage-like rectangle that you place on your upper arm, abdomen, back, or butt weekly, which releases estrogen and progestin. You'll use a new one once a week for three weeks, and then go one week without it (during which you'll have your period). Be sure you don't put it somewhere where your clothes might rub it off—if it comes off, that's akin to skipping pills. The estrogen content you get from the patch is higher than that of pills, so if you are susceptible to blood clots, it's best to avoid this method.

Vaginal Ring

Containing both estrogen and progestin hormones, the ring is small and flexible, and can be used by inserting it into your vagina much like a tampon. You'll keep it in for three weeks, remove for a week (when you'll have your period), and then insert a new one. It's easy to use—there isn't a wrong way to put it in, and there's no way for it to get lost or move somewhere too high up. You shouldn't feel any discomfort, and it shouldn't get in the way of sex, although it can accidentally come out during sex—but rest assured, it can be removed for up to three hours at a time without changing its effectiveness. The dosage of hormones is lower than other methods of birth control, so if your body hasn't reacted well to higher dosages, this could be the ideal option for you. It's also one to consider if you don't want to have to remember to take a pill daily.

Contraceptive Injection

This is a shot that you get once every three months, containing only progestin and protecting you from pregnancy for twelve weeks after the injection. You'll likely experience irregular bleeding when you first start this method, but after about a year, most women have either very light or no periods at all. There's a two-week window of flexibility if you can't make it to a health center to get your next shot exactly three months later, but if you have trouble keeping track of the amount of time that's passed or aren't sure you'll be able to make it to the doctor regularly, this option might not be for you.

Is It Enough Just to Use a Condom?

If used correctly, condoms can effectively protect you from pregnancy and STDs. But there are too many mistakes that can happen with condoms to rely solely on them for protection; they can break or the wrong kind of lubricant can break them down, for example. To prevent pregnancy most effectively, use another form of contraception with a condom. And to ensure that you're being best protected from any STDs, stick with latex or polyurethane varieties—the lambskin ones won't provide the protection you need.

IUD

There are two main types of IUDs—one that contains copper and no hormones (which lasts up to twelve years), and one that releases progestin (effective for up to five years). The IUD is a small T-shaped mechanism, which a doctor will insert, with a one- or two-inch string that hangs down from the bottom. Since it's possible for the IUD to slip or move, especially in the beginning, you may want to check every few days to make sure you can still feel the string. Although it's nice to have an option where you're protected from pregnancy for years without having to think too much about it, you should have regular check-ups every couple of months to make sure everything looks fine. It's possible that you could get an infection during insertion, or it may push itself up through the wall of the uterus, which may require surgery to fix.

The Implant

This method requires a thin plastic rod (about the size of a matchstick) to be inserted into your arm. The implant releases progestin only and lasts for about three years. You won't be able to see the implant, but if you press against the area, you may be able to feel it.

When Do You Need to Use Emergency Contraception?

Mistakes happen—you wake up the morning after a hook-up, only to remember you had forgotten to take your birth control pill. Or you notice after the fact that the condom broke. Or you've left for a weekend trip and don't realize until the next morning that you left your birth control at home. Whatever the circumstances, realizing your method of protection fell through is a scary situation that can make any collegiette panic, but knowing what emergency contraception is and where you can get it should you ever need it can help you feel a little more at ease.

Even though it's known as the morning-after pill, it's important to note that you don't need to wait until morning to take it! If you had unprotected sex, you can take emergency contraception immediately after intercourse.

If you don't realize you need emergency contraception until later, or you don't have access to it for a few days, don't worry . . . too much. You can still take emergency contraception up to three days after intercourse and still have it protect you effectively, but it's best, of course, to take it as soon as you can.

The greatest misconception about the morning-after pill is that it's akin to an abortion pill. If fertilization has already occurred, the morning-after pill isn't going to work—so it doesn't actually stop a pregnancy. What it does is delay ovulation, or the release of the egg from the ovaries, which stops sperm from fertilizing it, *preventing* pregnancy—not terminating it.

Where to Get Birth Control

You already know how to get a typical prescription from your doctor (and how to fill it at the drugstore), but, believe it or not, you can buy certain contraceptives online, too. Here's where you can get birth control aside from the pharmacy, both in person and online.

Planned Parenthood

With hundreds of locations across the United States, Planned Parenthood offers various women's health services (offerings may differ from location to location, so call or check their website), and is a resource for birth control as well, both daily contraceptives and the emergency variety.

Family Planning Health Services (http://shop.fphs.org)

Can't get to a drugstore to pick up Plan B? Or maybe you don't need it urgently, but are looking to keep some on hand, just in case? You can buy it online. Just make sure you take into account shipping time so you get it when you need it.

Getting Tested for STDs

Condoms, the pill, visits to the gynecologist—despite all the precautions you take to ensure you have safe sex, if you're hooking up with different guys or if your significant other (SO) has a sexual history, you are exposing yourself to risk.

Even though STDs are the least sexy thing to think about when you're getting hot and heavy with the guy in the dorm next door, make sure you're taking *every* precaution: That means being on the pill or some other form of regular birth control as well as using a condom to protect from STDs. And remember, you can contract STIs and STDs from oral sex, too—so unless you are using a condom or a dental dam, know that you are exposing yourself to the possibility of an infection.

If you're sexually active with a regular partner, bring up the conversation of safe sex—not just in the context of the act of sex (such as using a condom), but also getting tested, particularly if either of you has had past partners. Knowing both of you have tested negative for all STIs and STDs will give you peace of mind (so you can actually enjoy the time you spend together!), and if either of you does have something that could be passed on to the other, you can be extra careful in taking steps not to let that happen.

What Are Some of the Most Common STIs/STDs Found on Campus?

Chlamydia

Most people who have chlamydia may not show symptoms. If your symptoms do show, however, here's what you should look out for: pain during sex, irregular menstrual bleeding, lower abdominal pain, unusual vaginal discharge, and fever or nausea. Fortunately, chlamydia is easily treated with antibiotics, and you should abstain from sex during treatment.

Gonorrhea

You might have gonorrhea if you have pain or a burning sensation when urinating, or if you have to pee often. You'll also feel pain during sex and have spotting between periods. Like chlamydia, this can be treated with antibiotics.

Herpes

You can catch genital herpes as well as oral herpes through intercourse or oral sex. It's highly contagious, and symptoms generally appear a few weeks after sex. The first symptom you'll have is pain or itching, and you may also develop small red bumps and blisters or even open sores around the genital area. Someone who doesn't show symptoms may still be carrying the infection. Your doctor will provide you antiviral medications to treat herpes, and since herpes may continue to crop up over the course of your life, your doctor may also provide you with a prescription for additional medications you can take in the instance of flare-ups.

To better protect yourself from STDs, in addition to using condoms and other forms of protection when applicable, wash your genital area with soap and try to pee after you have sex; both will help flush out any nasty germs before they have a chance to infect you (don't forgo other forms of protection because you're counting on this!). Don't douche (a method of cleaning out the vagina using water or a cleansing solution)—doing so may actually increase your risk of catching an STI, because it disrupts the pH balance of your vagina, possibly clearing out the good bacteria you need to fight infection and disease.

How Do You Get Tested for STDs?

Getting tested is as simple as calling in to make an appointment at your doctor's office or simply getting a walk-in appointment at a free clinic, such as Planned Parenthood or your college's health center. Many campus health centers offer free STD testing on a regular basis, so check out their website or make a trip over there to find out the deal.

If you're visiting a clinic for the first time, it's a good idea to research the ones in your area beforehand: Check the reviews, decide if you want your doctor to be male or female, and check his or her credentials. It's your body, so you want to make sure you receive the best treatment that's most comfortable for you.

Depending on what you're being tested for, you may need to get a Pap smear, have your blood drawn, provide a urine sample, or have a swab of your vaginal fluids looked at. If any results come back positive, your doctor will provide you with the proper treatment, and even if it's difficult to do so, the responsible thing to do would be to share the information with any recent sexual partners. If you're concerned about confidentiality (as in, you're worried that your former flame or one-night stand might blab or not take it so well), try talking to a counselor at school about the best way to handle the situation.

Wellness Check-In: Five Ways to Stay on Top of Your Sexual Health

1. **Visit your gynecologist annually!** The exam will cover pretty much every women's health concern there is, so you'll know you're healthy inside and out.

2. **If you're sexually active, make sure you have a regular method of birth control.** If one type of pill or birth control doesn't work for you, you may need to go through a period of trial and error to find one that does work!

3. **Communicate with your partner!** The best way to stay healthy in a sexual relationship is to be open and honest with the other person about your concerns and about how you can both stay safe.

4. **Remember that people can carry STIs without showing symptoms,** so especially if you are hooking up with multiple people whose sexual histories you don't know, you should be getting checked regularly for infection or disease.

5.   **Better to be safe than sorry**—if you suspect your method of protection may not have been totally reliable, get an emergency contraceptive!

Chapter Checklist

✓ Be prepared with what to expect when you visit the gyne-cologist. It can be an uncomfortable experience, so don't be afraid to be picky when choosing your doctor, and make sure you're seeing someone you feel you can trust completely.

✓ Always be honest with your doctor. This goes for all health concerns, but since subjects concerning sex can feel a little more personal and sensitive, here is where you might feel like withholding some information. Your doctor needs to know everything in order to treat you to the best of her abil-ities, so she needs to know any relevant information, even if it's a little embarrassing to talk about.

✓ Be aware of the common conditions that affect women, and know what the symptoms are so you can get to your doc-tor right away if necessary. As with all medical issues, early detection is the best way to get successful treatment.

✓ Consider all birth control options before choosing one; think about your lifestyle (for example, if you're too busy to remember to take a pill every day) as well as any medical conditions (such as if you're prone to migraines or might be at greater risk for blood clots) that may point you towards a certain birth control method.

✓ Know where to get birth control and emergency contracep-tives, both in person and online.

✓ If you're sexually active, you are at risk of contracting an STI, even with protection, so be sure to get tested. Be able to recognize the signs of common STIs so you know if you need medical treatment immediately.

PART 3

Developing Smart and Successful Relationships

U p until the day you leave for college, the relationships in your life remain relatively constant: You have your family, whom you've known your entire life; you have your friends from school, whom you see every day (and whose secrets and awkward stages you remember like the back of your hand); and you have the random assortment of friends you've picked up from odd jobs, summer camp, sports teams, and travel, most of whom get to know you in some kind of structured, supervised setting.

The second you show up on campus your first day of freshman year, however, everything changes. You're constantly meeting new people: your roommate, your classmate, your professors, your crush, and so many more. Not a single one of those new people knows anything about your past; about what you were like when you were thirteen and awkward; about the hard times you've been through or the fabulous, quirky traits you have that are totally endearing (at least, you think so). You have to get to know them without all of that history, which can be a fantastic fresh start, albeit a challenging one at times. We've got you covered with the tips, tricks, and advice you need to navigate all kinds of college relationships, from your dorm room to the classroom and back again!

CHAPTER 10

Roommates

Whether you're an incoming freshman dreaming about dorm life or a seasoned collegiette looking forward to moving in with her bestie, you're bound to encounter all of the ups and downs of roomie life. For some, sharing space with a roommate is more of a roller coaster than smooth sailing, but that doesn't mean you can't have the best time ever in your dorm, provided you and your roomie work together to make the space a peaceful one! Learn what to expect of your random roomie or your BFF, how to bond, how to deal with conflict, and why creating a roommate contract could be the best decision you ever make in college. Who knows? You and your roomie could become a dynamic duo to rival Rachel and Monica!

HOW TO BOND WITH YOUR ROOMMATE

Say what you will, but getting a new roommate is always nerve-racking. As your move-in date gets closer and closer, you start asking yourself a million questions: Will your roomie's mess penetrate your personal space bubble? Are you going to be sexiled every weekend? Will your roommate be able to tolerate your less-than-normal sleeping habits? Most importantly, will the two of you become friends, or will the room be plagued by a perpetual awkward silence? Unless you're a lone wolf, you'll definitely prefer the former. Easier said than done, right? Not necessarily. Try some of these fun ways to bond with your new roomie.

Go to Dinner

Try a new restaurant with your roommate or simply find time to meet in the dining hall—you can spend hours together trying to figure out what type of meat the "meatloaf" is.

Go Exploring

Walk around campus with your roommate on a nice day before classes begin and find all the buildings where your courses will be. Figuring out where to go (without the pressure of getting to lecture on time) can ease your first-day-of-class nerves. Once you find your classes, stroll by the dining halls, student union, and fitness center.

Attend Orientation Activities

During orientation, your school will hold a variety of events and activities that'll help you jump into campus life. Explore the club fair (which showcases all the student-run clubs) and attend school- or club-sponsored events with your roomie.

Decorate Your Room

Once you both have your own belongings unpacked and set up, talk about what you could do to bring your individual spaces together. There are tons of cute dorm ideas on Pinterest that you can look to for crafty inspiration.

Create a Goal List for the Year

The two of you can write down your top ten goals for the school year and post them on your minifridge or door. For optimal bonding, make sure to support each other in working toward those goals!

Host a Movie Night

Have a chick flick night every so often to just relax and unwind from studying. Though we can't *guarantee* that you and your roomie will be a modern-day version of Rachel and Monica—because that was so long ago—we will tell you one thing: Chances are your roommate wants to get to know you just as much as you want to get to know her! Even if the two of you don't reach BFF status, you'll feel a million times better once you've established a healthy roomie relationship.

TIPS FOR ROOMING WITH A FRIEND

So, you're about to move in with your BFF—does life get any better than this? You think not; you couldn't be happier! From the day you signed your housing agreement, you knew that roommate horror stories wouldn't happen to you ever again (or at all, if you're an incoming freshman).

However, living with your BFF might not be quite as effortless as hanging out with her. If you don't take the time to set boundaries and outline a few rules now, your roommate/BFF could become your roommate/ex-BFF—and fast. Follow these friendship-saving steps and living with your bestie will be smooth sailing this year!

Set Ground Rules

When you live with someone, you will always learn new things about her, no matter *how* well you knew her before. Maybe she cuts her toenails in the middle of your dorm room floor. Maybe she's a stickler when it comes to quiet hours. Maybe she sings "Bootylicious" whenever she gets ready in the morning. Unfortunately, there's no way to make this adjustment process gradual; like it or not, from move-in day on you will be bombarded with your BFF-turned-roommate's habits, and she with yours.

Living with your bestie is going to bring on almost as many surprises as living with a stranger would, but unlike moving in with a rando, moving in with your BFF gives you a head start on communication. Take the time to set ground rules before the semester begins—it'll be so much easier to make concessions with her than it would be with a total stranger.

After you've moved your boxes into your new place, take a look around and say to your BFF, "Hey, I think it'd be great if we could sit down for ten minutes and chat about our expectations for this place, and set a few ground rules. This way we can avoid having minor conflicts blow up into huge fights!"

Here are some good points to bring up in this conversation:

- Will we be borrowing each other's clothes? Do we have open closets, or should we ask first before borrowing something?
- Will we be sharing food, or using separate shelves?
- Who will clean what?
- How will we handle visitors (especially overnight ones)?
- What does your course load look like this semester? What is your schedule like?
- How will I know when you need some alone time?

While having this conversation won't prevent *all* conflicts, it gives you and your BFF an idea of how to be respectful of each other's needs. Just remember: While these rules are a way to ease yourselves into your new living situation, they aren't set in stone. Prepare to be flexible throughout the year, and adjust your rules (pending a discussion with your roommate) if your habits begin to get on each other's nerves.

Communicate, Communicate, Communicate

One way to minimize tensions that arise in your living space is to communicate vocally. If you feel your toes are being stepped on, don't be afraid to reach out (respectfully) to your bestie before whatever is bothering you drives a wedge between the two of you. And no matter how uncomfortable you feel telling your BFF that something she does bothers you (you never had problems before!), you need to talk to her face-to-face. This means no angry texts and no nasty messages on the whiteboard! Even though your roommate knows you well, she won't be able to read your passive-aggressive messages much better than anyone else will.

Poor communication between you and your bestie can mess with your social life, both inside *and* outside your dorm room. Rooming with your best friend usually means rooming with someone from your main group of friends, and drama with her could mean drama with *everyone*. So please, future BFF-roommate, always keep these words in the back of your mind: *I will not internalize my roommate grievances. I will not leave angry messages on Post-it notes. I will not give my roommate the cold shoulder. I will tell her, calmly, what bothers me. Later, when we're old ladies, we will laugh about this!*

Grow Separately Without Growing Apart

A wise woman once said, "The most beautiful discovery true friends make is that they can grow separately without growing apart." College is a major point in your life where you and your bestie may do just as this quote suggests: grow separately. But how do you make sure you don't grow apart?

Expand your social circles. We're not talking about Google+, here; we're talking about getting out and doing things with people besides your roommate, even though she's your best friend. Your roommate/bestie can quickly become your only friend if you don't put in the effort to branch out. Besides, the more you branch out, meet new people, and try new things, the more you'll have to chat about when you hang out again together in the room! So join a club your roommate's uninterested in or start playing Ultimate Frisbee on the quad with friends while your roomie's at crew practice; you'll only have more to talk about when you get home.

In the meantime, don't forget to plan special roomie sessions with your BFF, like Sunday dinners or Netflix binge-watching nights. This way, no matter how busy your individual plans keep you, there will always be room for each other in your schedules.

Coming home to your BFF's familiar face can be comforting, but it takes hard work to maintain that comfort. By laying your expectations on the table in the first place; accepting the fact that conflict is inevitable; employing direct, respectful communication; and making time for both personal growth and bonding, you will become the best BFF roommate you can be. Let the late-night study sessions and pizza runs begin!

Unspoken Rule of Dorm Life #1:
Don't Keep Your Door Shut All the Time

No one will want to introduce him- or herself to the person who's always locked in her room, and sooner or later, you could start to find the building pretty lonely, no matter how many neighbors you have. Leave your door propped open so that people passing by can say hello and you can actually meet the people you're living alongside. Plus, with your door open, you'll be better able to hear whenever people are hanging in the common room, which means you'll know when to pop out and socialize during your study breaks!

HOW TO HANDLE ROOMMATE CONFLICTS

After all is said and done, you and your roomie are going to face typical roommate conflicts, whether you're just getting to know each other or have been friends for ages. It's unavoidable, and it definitely isn't the end of the world! The important thing is knowing how to handle issues so that they don't escalate into major conflict and cause you extra stress.

Allow us to set the scene for you: It's the start of the semester, and you and your new roommate are all settled into your double (it may be the smallest one on your floor, but the two of you can make it work), or you've finally found someone who can cover half the rent on your off-campus apartment.

At first, everything is great! You're both super cautious about keeping the space clean, being quiet during sleeping hours and asking before you invite a campus cutie back to your place. But after a few weeks of stellar conduct, you may find yourself kicking your shoes off in the doorway or sneaking your boyfriend or girlfriend back to your room without telling your roomie first, or she may be doing it to you. It's no big deal, right?

Unfortunately, your roommate probably doesn't appreciate stumbling over your gym shoes, and you may not like listening to her clack away at her keyboard at ungodly hours of the night. So how do you deal? Here are a few lifestyle differences you might run into and how to cope with them.

She's Super Messy

You've been taught to make your bed first thing every morning and to fold your clothes straight out of the laundry before putting them away neatly. Your roommate, on the other hand, leaves clothes strewn across her bed, which remains perpetually unmade. There's trash everywhere, but thankfully only on her side of the room.

This is perhaps the most iconic example of roommate clashes. An unmade bed can be unsightly to someone who loves cleanliness, but it can be equally difficult for a girl who's oblivious to messes to suddenly get the urge to clean.

How to Deal

If you have a need for clean, try to keep it to your side of the room. Your roommate is not under your control, and you cannot expect her to conform to your standards. It only becomes a real issue—an issue you can call her out on—if her mess spreads into your shared space, or worse, your personal space. If the room gets smelly or grimy, that's another sign you can speak your mind and try to work it out.

Suggest making a chore schedule. No one *likes* forcing herself to do chores, but trust us, you'll be thankful you did it! A cleaning schedule is a great way to divide responsibilities and make sure that your room is clean on a regular basis. It's best to come up with the schedule early in the year so you can stick to it—no excuses!

If the problem gets to be more serious, consider approaching your roommate about it again. Remind her that it's your space, too, and it's her responsibility to help keep it looking nice. If the problem gets way out of hand and your roommate gets angry or aggressive about it, consider taking the problem to your RA or another member of Residence Life. They're there to help you with housing and roommate issues, so take advantage of their assistance.

She's Up When You're Sleeping

One of you likes to get up with the sun, while the other loves burning the midnight oil. We all have our own circadian rhythms that are hard to reprogram. It's equally frustrating for her to try to sleep with the lights on as it is for you to hear her alarm blaring hours before you're slated to wake up.

How to Deal

If you're finding your sleep habits are causing tension, there may be a way to get back in sync! Get a sleep mask to keep the light out of your eyes and earplugs to block the sound of the alarm. Try to be as quiet as possible in the early mornings if your roommate sleeps late, or do your late-night studying in your dorm's common room if you're the night owl. Try to be respectful of your roomie's sleeping times. After all, being wakened in the middle of a good dream is perhaps the worst thing ever.

She's Absent

When you pictured your dorm, you may have imagined yourself and your roomie hanging out, eating snacks, and watching chick flicks every night. While that's not a completely impossible scenario, it's not always the reality. Enter the MIA roomie, who simply doesn't seem to exist. Sometimes girls practically move into someone else's room or spend all of their time off campus, coming back only to grab clothes or when drama erupts between them and their friends.

Absent roommates can be tricky, as they're usually absent for their own reasons. Some girls get invested in their new significant others, make friends in a different building, or are simply too busy to hang around the room. There's nothing wrong with a busy roommate, but it can be kind of a bummer hanging out by yourself when you come home from class!

How to Deal

If your roommate's absence bothers you, try inviting her to hang out on the off days when she does come back to the room. Ask her what she's been up to lately. If she's not giving much of an answer, don't pry, but do be wary. You want to make sure she's not getting herself into any kind of trouble!

If you're truly worried about your roomie and where she might be, encourage her to talk with your RA. She could be getting into a sticky situation with a controlling boyfriend or girlfriend or staying out too late and crashing at other people's rooms who don't actually want her there.

She's Always in the Room

While having a roommate who's never there can be a bummer, so can having a roommate who's constantly in the room. It's always fun to have some roomie bonding time, but you'll need a break from each other once in a while. It's called alone time, and you might go nuts without it! Trust us: It's easy to get sick of each other when you're sharing a small space for at least a whole school year!

How to Deal

If your roommate is in your room around the clock (except for class time), you might want to have a chat with her. It could be that she's simply not involved in anything else or doesn't have many other friends, so encourage her to branch out and commit to something on campus. Clubs, organizations, sports, or on-campus jobs can be a great way to spend your time, get involved, and meet new people (more on that in Chapter 14). Meeting new people means making friends, and having friends means having a social life outside of the dorm room! It's a win-win: Your roomie will find some besties, and you'll have some much-needed, solo rest time in the room.

If, on the other hand, your roommate is simply more introverted and isn't looking to meet new people, steer her toward the library or student lounges on campus for studying. Remind her that there are plenty of other places on campus to hang out and get work done. If it's necessary, remind her that your shared room belongs to you as well, and that you'd appreciate having the space to yourself once in a while.

She Always Has People Over

"The more the merrier" isn't always true, especially when it comes to sharing a relatively small space. Unfortunately, some roommates don't think about this and bring in friends and significant others to hang out—*all of the time.* Worse still, they don't always ask (or warn) you that you'll be having company, so it can throw your plans and your rest and relaxation (or study) time way out of whack.

How to Deal

It's always polite to ask! If someone's going to be in your room other than you, let your roomie know in advance, and ask her to do the same for you.

If your roommate seems to have people over all the time without telling you, however, talk to her about it. As with so many other roomie problems, communication is key. While you might feel a little awkward telling your roommate to not invite her friends over, or even asking her to essentially kick them out of the room, she has to realize that your room is a shared space. If you're having trouble coming to an agreement, look at your schedules and find a way to fit in times or days where it's acceptable to have guests. For example, let her know that she'll have the room to herself and is free to have friends over if and when you go home for the weekend. The night before a huge exam, on the other hand? Probably not.

She Puts Her Sex Life on Display (or Constantly Sexiles You)

It can be pretty awkward trying to study while your roommate is spending some quality time with her significant other ten feet away from you. Especially when it's, you know, *quality* time.

Believe it or not, it's pretty common for collegiettes to get caught in that awkward "Don't they even know I'm here?!" moment that accompanies a roommate getting busy, whether it's a late night (and she assumes you're sleeping) or a time when she's unaware that you're even in the room (curse those top-bunk beds!). Even more common is the sexiling experience—when your roommate exiles you from the room so she can hook up—which poses all kinds of other problems: namely, where you'll be sleeping. Can't a collegiette catch a break?

How to Deal

Talk to your roommate to find a solution that works for you when it comes to hooking up in the room. See if she'll shoot you a text when someone is coming over so that you have time to make other arrangements if necessary, or if you can agree to certain times or days of the week when overnight visitors are allowed (e.g., no one can stay the night on weeknights).

If your roommate is someone who either has an SO or frequently enjoys bringing home her flings, it's essential that you establish a reliable place that you can crash for the night. Whether it's with one of your friends or your own guy, having a backup place to sleep is necessary in college. There's nothing more uncomfortable than having to sleep someplace like the study lounge. Or even worse, insisting on staying in your room and trying to fall asleep to the hook-up noises emanating from a bed that is literally only five feet away from you. Not. Ideal.

She Uses Your Stuff All of the Time

For some new college students, having a roommate is like having the sister they never had growing up: double the closet space, sleepovers every night, and tons of clothes to share. For others, a roommate is just a roommate, and their belongings are personal, not to be shared or borrowed. No matter how you treat your property and privacy, you should make sure your roommate is on the same page.

How to Deal

As soon as you've settled in, you should discuss boundaries with your roommate. This could even be done while you're crafting your roommate contract (more on that later!) or cleaning schedule. Make sure you tell her specifically what you're comfortable sharing, whether it's clothing or even chairs (some girls won't want you to sit on theirs). Everyone treats her own privacy and property differently, so make sure to remain open-minded and respectful!

If a borrowing issue arises as the semester continues, you'll have to address it. When she borrows a scarf off the back of your chair for a day, simply mention that you'd rather she not do that. If she repeatedly goes through your belongings to pick out her favorite things to borrow, you may want to consider having a more serious conversation about boundaries. If the issue persists even after the conversation, take it to an RA, who can help mediate.

Unspoken Rule of Dorm Life #2: There Is No Complaining on Thursdays, Fridays, and Saturdays

If people are playing music too loudly, talking too loudly, or generally distracting you with their revelry on the weekends, well, you'll just have to deal. It's the weekend, and absolutely no one cares if you want to study. The noise won't dissipate anytime soon (but you can bet it'll die down Sunday afternoon), and since there are rarely ever any designated dorm quiet hours on weekends, any complaints will fall on deaf ears. Hey, if you can't beat 'em, join 'em—you might even make some new friends! If you really can't put your books down to join in, march yourself to the library.

ROOMMATE CONTRACTS

Tackling roommate conflicts can be about as fun as tackling that mammoth history essay you have on your to-do list (read: not super fun), but you can avoid a lot of those awkward conversations by setting some ground rules right off the bat. If you establish expectations on day one, you'll encounter a lot less confusion and conflict down the line. The best way to do it? Create a roommate contract!

What's a Roommate Contract?

A roommate contract is an agreement (usually a written one) that helps you and your roommate settle on rules you'll both follow throughout the year. Roommate contracts can take numerous forms and are sometimes required for all students living in a dorm. Check out our sample roommate contract at the end of this chapter!

What Should Be Included?

A good roommate contract should address both of the roommates' preferences on how the space will be used and general rules for the room. Things to think about including in your roommate contract are:

- How you'll handle distractions that could interfere with studying (music, TV, friends, etc.)
- "Quiet hours" when you want to sleep or study
- How clean the room should be and regular cleaning times
- When it's okay to have people over and how many people can be over at a time
- Rules for anything you two will share in the room (TV, fridge, microwave, etc.)
- When you need to lock the door and how long the room can be left unlocked
- If the door will remain open or shut when one or both of you is in the room
- What will happen if a guy comes back to the room and if you can kick each other out or not
- How hot or cold the room should be and when the windows can be open
- Steps for resolving fights or arguments
- What you can borrow or take from each other's sides of the room (food, clothes, etc.)

Keep in mind that you and your roommate can make changes throughout the year as well if unexpected conflicts arise. Discuss them with each other, notify your RA if necessary, and make sure each of you gets an updated version of the contract.

I Want to Make One! How Do I Explain It to My Roommate?

If you're not living somewhere that requires roommate agreements but are still interested in having one, you might try one of the following strategies to make your proposal a little less awkward.

Show Her This Chapter!

Talk to her next time she gets back to the room or leave this book open on her desk with a Post-it note that says something like, "Saw this and thought it was a good idea. Want to give it a try?"

Provide Examples

Use other schools to provide context. Bring up the idea of a contract and focus on how other schools require it. It must be a necessity at institutions like Case Western Reserve University and FIT for a reason, right? By providing examples of where it's worked, you will have an easier time selling her on the idea.

Wait until You Meet Her

Sit down over one of your first lunches or dinners back on campus to see how different the two of you actually are. Both of you have 8 A.M. classes? Maybe a contract won't be necessary. See what the first few days are like so you have specific examples of things you feel a contract would be helpful towards before suggesting one.

Focus on the Mutual Benefits

Emphasize the fact that the contract will benefit both of you. Make sure she knows that you don't just want to make a roommate agreement to prevent her from annoying you, but you also want to make sure you don't do anything that bugs her.

What Happens When My Roommate or I Break the Contract?

Consequences can vary based on whether or not a roommate contract was required and who oversaw the process. If your RA is aware that you and your roommate have an agreement or if he helped you set it up, let him know and get his help resolving any issues that pop up.

When a roommate contract violation occurs, be honest and upfront about it. If you're the one who violated it, ask your roommate to sit down and discuss the violation if necessary. If your roommate was the one who violated the agreement, follow the same procedure. You can decide if you want to edit or change the contract to prevent a similar problem from occurring again, or if there's some way to enforce things a bit better.

If a problem or roommate contract violation is super serious, your RA is always a good person to go to, even if he didn't help you create the agreement. He can help you reach a fair solution and find ways to keep the problem from happening again as well.

The Official Her Campus Roommate Contract

Roommate One: _____

Roommate Two: _____

Smoking will be allowed in the room: ○ Yes ○ No
Drinking will be allowed in the room: ○ Yes ○ No
   During these specific times: _____

These hours will be reserved for sleeping: _____

When one roommate is sleeping, the other roommate may:
   ○ Play music
   ○ Listen to music with headphones
   ○ Watch TV
   ○ Have guests over
   ○ Use a hair dryer
   ○ Have the lights on
   ○ Have a desk lamp on
   ○ Other: _____

These hours will be reserved for study time: _____

When one roommate is studying, these background activities may take place:

- ⭘ Music
- ⭘ TV
- ⭘ Friends over
- ⭘ Other: _____

We will keep our room   ⭘ Messy ⭘ In between ⭘ Neat

We will clean the room   ⭘ Daily ⭘ Weekly ⭘ Monthly

                                        ⭘ Other: _____

Our cleaning will include:

- ⭘ Doing laundry before the basket overflows
- ⭘ Washing dishes after using them
- ⭘ Taking out the trash and recycling once a week
- ⭘ Vacuuming once a week
- ⭘ Making our beds daily
- ⭘ Other: _____

During these hours, a roommate may have friends over:

_____, A roommate may have _____

_____ friends over at once.

Overnight guests are allowed: ⭘ Yes ⭘ No

Before a roommate has an overnight guest, she will warn the other roommate _____ **days in advance.**

How often may a roommate have an overnight guest?

_____

Roommate policy on overnight guests (e.g., if it is okay to request that the other roommate leave):

_____

_____

List of items that may be shared:

_____

_____

List of items that may NOT be shared:

_____

_____

List of items that may be shared as long as the roommate asks beforehand:

_____

_____

List of items that may be shared as long as the roommate replaces them/returns them as they were found:

_____

_____

The door will be locked:
- ○ When neither roommate is there
- ○ When one roommate is there
- ○ When both roommates are there
- ○ At these specific times: _____

We will leave the door open:
- ○ When one person is in the room
- ○ When both of us are in the room
- ○ Never, the door will always be shut
- ○ Under these circumstances: _____

The windows may be open during these times: _____

An acceptable temperature range for the room during the day is:

_____

An acceptable temperature range for the room during the night is:

_____

In the case of an argument, we will:

_____

_____

In the case of a violation of this contract, we will:

_____

_____

Additional items to consider:

_____

_____

Signed,

X_____ [Roommate One] _____

X_____ [Roommate Two] _____

X_____ [Resident Advisor] _____

While your experience sharing a room may not always go smoothly, it will, all in all, be rewarding. As long as you're communicating effectively with your roommate and letting her know about any issues that arise, your relationship shouldn't suffer. Roommate bonds are like no other relationship and can last a lifetime, so don't let silly little habits get in the way of an awesome friendship!

Sticky Situation: You Don't Want to Live with Your Current Roommate Next Year

If you want to break it off and find yourself a more compatible roommate for the future (like that bestie from your psych class you just click with), you should explain it in person, just like any other relationship. Give your roomie plenty of notice so that she can make other plans. No matter what your level of frustration may be, it's important to approach the discussion in a calm and understanding way. You don't have to go into why you don't want to live with her next year—just say that you're trying to make the best decision for you. No feelings hurt, and everyone gets something that works out for her.

Wellness Check-In: Five Ways You and Your Roommate Can Keep Each Other Healthy

As awesome as it is that you're living it up at your new college (no longer worried about curfews, veggies at dinner, or daily vitamins, like your parents always pressed on you), you may find that your newfound freedom makes it a lot more difficult to stay on top of your health, both physical and mental. Your roommate might be the closest thing you have to family, given that you live together, and that means you might be each other's best motivators when it comes to keeping healthy. Take advantage of that built-in support system and get started!

Take an Exercise Class Together

Instead of hitting the gym alone, ask your roommate if she wants to sign up for an exercise class with you. Some colleges even offer gym classes for credit, and since you won't have to worry about a water aerobics midterm, you'll be killing two birds with one athletic stone.

Share a Stock of Sick-Day Essentials

Having a communal box of remedies at the ready means you'll be ready to stave off even the worst headaches or common colds or treat any injuries you might get (say, falling off the top bunk or banging your knee against the side of your desk).

What you might want in your stash:

- Ibuprofen
- Acetaminophen
- Menstrual symptom relief medication
- Decongestants
- Allergy medication

- Vitamin C
- A thermometer
- Cough drops
- Adhesive bandages
- A first aid kit
- Antiseptic cleanser
- Antibiotic ointment

Shop for Healthy Snacks Together

To motivate yourself to eat healthy in and out of your dorm room, take a trip to the on-campus one-stop-shop or an off-campus grocery store with your roommate and agree to both stock up on healthy snacks for the room.

Use the Buddy System

The buddy system may seem like a back-to-basics approach circa preschool, but it actually has its advantages in college. Make your roomie your buddy (for real), and you can be hers. Look out for each other, keeping an eye on each other's sobriety (or drunkenness) and traveling together to any parties; that way, if one of you starts to go overboard or if you end up in a sketchy situation, your buddy can bail you out and get you back home safely! You'll also find even more tips on staying safe on campus in Part 1.

Be Honest with Each Other

At the end of the day, you're not your roommate's mom, nor is she yours. Still, if you feel that your roommate is heading down a bad path, you should speak up. Whether she's surrounding herself with bad company, developing bad habits, or falling into a freshman-year funk, it's something you need to address for her health and safety's sake. The best roomies look out for each other, and that means helping each other with life's ups and downs and involving RAs if any kind of serious intervention is necessary. Check out Chapter 8 for more tips on helping a friend who is going through a tough time.

Chapter Checklist

✓ Connect with your soon-to-be roomie on social media or Skype, but don't judge a book by its cover or jump to conclusions about how well you'll get along.

✓ Bond with your roomie by hitting up the dining hall or orientation festivities, and make your dorm room décor a team effort!

✓ If you're living with a friend, be sure to set ground rules first so you're on the same page about important things like chores, quiet hours, guests, and more.

✓ No matter what conflict you and your roommate are facing, always communicate openly (and face-to-face!) about it. Work together to come up with a compromise—the room belongs to both of you, so you should both have a say in how you use and treat it.

✓ Consider making a roommate contract to prevent any miscommunications down the road. Involve your RA to make it official!

✓ Treat the room the way you would want your roommate to treat it; you won't be able to call her out on her messy habits if you're also messy without coming off as a hypocrite!

✓ Your roommate could become the closest thing you have to family at college, so look out for each other's safety and overall well-being!

CHAPTER 11

Professors, RAs, and TAs

As important as it is to know what to expect from your roomie, it may be even more important to go into college with an understanding of your superiors, such as your professors, RAs, and TAs. Sure, they aren't the ones lounging with you while you indulge in Netflix marathons or wax poetic about the guy you're crushing on from down the hall, but they still play a huge role in your college experience, from dorm life to academics. Knowing how to handle those relationships and make the most of them is one of the most important lessons you'll learn at school—after all, these individuals are not only some of your best on-campus resources, but also potentially your biggest cheerleaders and allies!

RESIDENT ASSISTANTS

Ah, resident assistants. The title just sounds so collegiate and official, doesn't it? Affectionately known as RAs, resident assistants are your ultimate resources for everything dorm: They're the ones who give you all the info you need on move-in day, gather you and your new floormates together for bonding activities, let you back into your room when you've lost your key (which will happen many, many times), lend you an ear and advice when you're feeling homesick or dealing with roomie conflicts, and direct you to other on-campus resources when you're in a bind (such as the counseling office, academic services, and more). The best thing about RAs is that they get you—usually they're only one or two years older than you are, which means they know how you feel.

Sadly, RAs can sometimes get a bad rap because they're always enforcing rules, like busting you for violating quiet hours. In reality, your RA is just looking out for you—that's his or her job!

When to Go to Them

Don't just let your RA play disciplinarian; it's not the best way to utilize her as a resource, and it's definitely not how your RA wants to be spending her time, either. Instead, make your RA/resident relationship a positive one!

Stop by your RA's room during the first week of classes to formally introduce yourself (she will probably remember you from your floor's welcoming meeting, but a one-on-one hello is much more personal). Most RAs abide by an open-door policy or have hours written on their doors showing when they're available, so you shouldn't worry about imposing!

You can also go to your RA with serious concerns. Feeling homesick? Your RA can talk it out with you. Got a conflict in your dorm room? Your RA can mediate a convo between you and your roomie to work it out or can bring in higher-ups to work out a transfer. Have a friend who's struggling with emotional issues or a serious drinking problem, and unsure how to help? If all else fails and you're truly worried, your RA can help you and your friend find the resources she may need to get better (and the same applies if you're encountering those problems yourself!).

Your RA is there to help you; however, you should also be aware that colleges usually require RAs to follow a mandatory policy wherein they need to report anything they hear that could endanger the health of a student, be it underage drinking, harmful behaviors, or other issues. If anything else, that should motivate you to use your best judgment with all your activities, whether you're reporting something to your RA or not, because you don't want to wind up in a sticky or unsafe situation!

PROFESSORS

While resident assistants have the biggest influence over your dorm life at college, your professors definitely have the most control over your academic life, which means you need to get to know them (and get along with them!). You'll have all kinds of professors in college: the wizened old historian who shares fabulous stories of ye olde days; the earthy-crunchy environmental guru who makes you want to be one with nature (or roll your eyes, depending); the distracted professor who writes two notes on the board and rambles the rest of the class period; the young, devastatingly handsome philosophy professor; and so many more. Whatever type you're dealing with, you'll need to build a solid relationship with them in order to succeed!

How to Get to Know Your Professors

There are countless academic differences between high school and college, including the rigor of your courses and a different scheduling style, but one of the changes that could take the most getting used to is your class size and dynamic (especially at a larger school).

In high school, your classes hovered between fifteen and thirty-five students, but now you might find yourself stepping into lecture halls that look more like athletic arenas and sitting in class next to 300 of your peers. The professor might lecture using a podium or microphone, and when you raise your hand to speak, you just get pointed at instead of named. You may even use a buzzer to answer questions! You may wonder how you're ever going to get to know any of your professors, not to mention how you're going to get to know one well enough to ask for a recommendation from him or her down the road (senior year comes quickly).

However, you're not completely out of luck. Though it may require more effort on your part, there are some ways you can get to know your professors, even in a class of hundreds of students, and earn a killer recommendation down the road.

Don't Rush Out the Door after Class Ends

If you're not in a hurry to make it to another class, those few minutes after your lecture is over are a great time to introduce yourself to your professor or chat with her briefly. The lecture will be fresh in both of your minds, so you could easily ask her a question about something you didn't understand or talk about your opinion on an issue she mentioned.

This not only puts a face to your name for the professor, but it also shows her that you were actively paying attention to the lecture and that you cared enough about what she taught to talk about it even after class is over. Can you say brownie points?

Go to Office Hours, Even If You Don't Need Help

A common misconception about office hours is that they're only there for students struggling in the class who need extra help. While office hours are a great resource for getting your questions and concerns dealt with one-on-one, they're also a great way to get to know your professors! You can share your interests, get their insights, and become more memorable; that way, you can turn to them if you find yourself struggling in the future (or if things are going well and you'd like a letter of recommendation for an internship, job, or study abroad opportunity)! Besides, your professor will really appreciate your taking the time and initiative to establish that working relationship. You may not develop a Harry Potter/Dumbledore-esque relationship (dare to dream), but you could come close!

Seven Questions to Ask Your Professor During Office Hours

1. What made you want to teach this class?
2. What's the most important thing I can take away from this class?
3. How would you ask us about this topic on an exam?
4. How can I improve my grade?
5. Are there any on-campus resources you'd suggest I look into, such as tutors or study groups?
6. I didn't quite understand X in class. Can you explain it to me again?
7. I really love this subject. Are there any opportunities for me to get more involved in it on or off campus?

Take Advantage of Opportunities Outside of the Classroom

Many schools, both large and small, urge students to build relationships with their professors and even have programs and events to facilitate these relationships. Our favorite example? Many schools have "Take Your Professor to Lunch" programs where students can sign up for free meal vouchers to treat their professors to on-campus meals (and, you know, eat for free, which is always awesome). The idea of the program is to push students to spend time outside of class getting to know their professors, and with a free meal on the table, it's no surprise that these programs are catching on at colleges across the country.

Another great way to get to know a professor is to ask whether he's accepting any students for research programs, especially if he's a professor in the sciences. Private research is a great way to build a relationship with your professor, and it's also a great way for your professor to get a closer look at your work and interest in the subject matter, which could turn into great material for a recommendation in the future.

Lots of professors either conduct school-sponsored research projects during the semester or conduct their own research privately in concentrations of their own interest; you could join them! Many schools have listings for research opportunities online, but approaching your professor and just asking is an easy way to find out exactly what you want to know!

Stay in Touch

Even if you're not currently enrolled in that professor's class, it could still be beneficial to you in the long run to maintain your relationship with him or her and check back in every so often. Your professors will appreciate that you took the time to think about them and shoot a quick e-mail, which will not only keep you in their good graces if you ever need a recommendation, but will also keep you fresh in their minds! A professor will have a hard time writing a thoughtful and accurate recommendation for a student he hasn't taught or even spoken to in a few semesters. Send your professor an e-mail every now and then to stay connected.

Other good ways to keep in touch with your professors are to attend a lecture, talk, or presentation that they might be giving at school. The end of the program is a great chance to stop and talk to your prof—tell him how much you enjoyed his presentation and how you'd love to grab coffee to discuss it further sometime.

Another super easy tip? Take a class with your former professor again! Professors love seeing students who come back for more of their teaching, and the fact that they've already taught you gives you a head start on material for a rec because they've already seen how you work!

With these tips, you're bound to build great relationships with your professors. When you do ask for a recommendation, don't forget to ask politely—in-person beats e-mail any day, and be sure to give your teachers enough of a heads-up on the deadline so that they're not overwhelmed or scrambling to piece a recommendation together. And once you score that rec and land a killer job or internship with it, don't forget to send a thank-you note!

Things You Do That Make Professors Mad
- Ask a question that's answered on the syllabus
- Ask a question someone else just asked
- Eat or open food loudly during class
- Fidget
- Whisper to your neighbor
- Fail to take any notes
- Make a big deal out of going to the bathroom
- Don't bring the required materials to class
- Text in class
- Show up two minutes late—every time
- Ask for a recommendation the day before it's due

How to Talk Your Way to a Better Grade (When You Think You Deserve It)

When you know the quality of your work on an assignment wasn't your best, you usually expect the grade to be lower than normal. But what if your grade doesn't accurately reflect what you think you deserve? Maybe you thought your essay was right on point, but you got a D. Or maybe you thought you explained your answers clearly on the midterm exam, but the professor had other thoughts.

There are ways to deal with these situations other than venting on the phone to your parents or marching straight to your advisor's office to report the teacher for unfair grading practices. No matter which class is frustrating you, we've got the best advice on how to handle some common bad-grade situations.

Situation #1: You Think You Should Have Gotten More Points on This Test Than Your Final Score Indicates

If you've looked over your graded test thoroughly and you absolutely cannot figure out how your 89 percent was given a D+ (maybe the curve was really high?), you may want to confront your professor. In some classes, professors will review the exam in a class session and explicitly state the grading policies, including the curve if there is one.

But that's not always the case. If your professor doesn't review the test in class, ask her if you can make an appointment to review the test together. Beforehand, remember to take fifteen minutes to quietly review the test on your own. Additionally, if a TA (teaching assistant—learn more about them later in this chapter!) graded the exam, it's important that you speak to him before you approach the professor. By going over the TA's head, you might offend him. Remember, you don't want to burn any bridges in an academic setting!

Speaking with a Professor about Any Academic Issue

When speaking with a professor about any issue, remember to be courteous and professional at all times. If the professor is clearly opposed to changing the grade, don't become annoyed or inconsiderate. *Never* try to change an answer on a test after it has already been handed back to you. Not only is this dishonest and against university policies, but many professors also photocopy exams before handing them back so you would get caught.

Situation #2: You Bombed the Midterm and Want a Way to Make Up for It

Sometimes midterms simply don't go as well as you had hoped. You might have been busy working on a project for another class and didn't have time to study, or you might have been slacking on keeping up with the reading. Regardless, failing one midterm can cause your grade to drop fast. Although you can't go back and retake your midterm, there are steps you can take to keep this from happening again.

Talk to your instructor to see how you can best study for your next exam. You'll show that you care about the class (which never fails to impress professors) and you'll learn some insider tips or info you would never have known about the upcoming test otherwise!

Luckily, many professors will count the final grade more than the midterm grade. If you're still worried, you can also ask the professor if there are any extra credit opportunities. Some professors might empathize with your situation and be willing to help you improve your grade. Though you can't count on this option, it never hurts to ask!

Situation #3: You Thought Your Essay Warranted a Higher Grade Than the One You Received

Some students dread essays because they believe professors grade them more subjectively than they would an exam. Though the lines blur a bit when it comes to grading essays, most professors follow a rubric. If they don't, you can request that they provide you with detailed criteria as to how they graded the essay.

Once again, the best way to approach a professor about an essay issue is by scheduling a meeting. But before you do, make sure you've read the rubric and grading criteria thoroughly. Maybe the rubric says the emphasis of the paper was to "persuade," but you simply "informed." Little nuances like these can cause even the best-written papers to receive bad grades.

When you meet with your professor, ask him respectfully to explain what could have been done better in the essay. This way, you'll know why he was dissatisfied, and you can address anything you think was overlooked. Sometimes you can earn yourself an extension to make improvements or a grade adjustment if you really argue your case well and prove you met expectations!

Situation #4: You Don't Think Your Cumulative Grade Is an Accurate Reflection of How You've Done on the Assignments in Your Class

In most classes, chances are you're turning in frequent assignments to professors and receiving feedback. Therefore, when you are getting mostly As on your assignments and you find out that you received a B in the course, this can be a cause for concern.

The likely situation is that you didn't have a clear understanding of how each assignment was graded. Double-check your syllabus to find out how each assignment was weighted, and if your calculations based on your past grades still don't match what you've received, bring it up to your professor.

Because the course will likely be finished by the time this issue occurs, the best way to get in contact with the professor is by sending her an e-mail. If you feel you need to discuss the matter, ask to set up either an in-person or a phone meeting. Although this likely will not result in your receiving a higher grade (unless the professor made a mistake), it serves as further proof that you should carefully read and follow the syllabus throughout the course to avoid this problem!

Ultimately, all of the solutions come back to approaching your professor and having an effective conversation with him or her about your concerns. You may be tempted to run straight to your academic advisor with a grade dispute, but many of these issues can be solved in a one-on-one meeting in office hours or after class. If you truly believe the professor is being unfair, and you've tried to resolve it through conversation, then you're justified in approaching your advisor. At the end of the day, however, your professors are there to help you, not hurt you, so make the experience as positive as possible!

TAS: WHO THEY ARE AND HOW THEY CAN HELP YOU

Though it's important to know how to deal with your professors when problems arise—whether with your grades, the course material, or anything else related to your classes—your professor isn't always the one who's controlling your GPA; at least, not entirely. If you're attending a larger university, teaching assistants (affectionately known as TAs) are often the middlemen between you and your professor, and they're sometimes the ones who are teaching and even grading.

Teaching assistants are usually graduate students, which means they're not much older than you. They exist to help the professor and to help you. In large lectures, it can be tricky for students to really grasp the material or ask questions of the professor, so classes are split up into smaller discussion groups or lab sections a couple of times a week to supplement that lecture. That's where your TA comes in! TAs run those smaller groups, acting as stand-in professors by answering questions and leading discussions. This is their way of training for a life as a professor or as an expert in the field that they're studying, plus a way to get paid while they attend grad school.

One of the pros of having a TA is getting the chance to ask more specific questions than you would in your giant lecture hall. One of the cons, of course, is that your TA—and not your professor—could be the one making or breaking your grade, depending on how skilled she is at teaching and how tough her grading style is. Though your TA probably isn't as knowledgeable or skilled as your professor (because she is younger), getting to work with a TA in a smaller class size could be just the help you need to ace the class!

Wellness Check-In: Five Reasons Building a Relationship with Your TA Is Worth It

You Can Ask Questions

The better you get to know your TA in your smaller group meetings, the more comfortable you'll be asking all of the questions you were too freaked out to ask in your 300-person lecture.

You Get Personalized Advice

When you do work in close proximity with others (namely, a small group and your TA), it becomes more obvious what you're excelling at and what you're having trouble with, and your TA will notice. Then she will swoop in to the rescue! You'll get personalized advice tailored to your needs.

You'll Be Recognized for Your Extra Effort

TAs are the ones who see you trying hard at your studies: asking good questions, improving in the classroom, and turning in everything on time. When it comes time for your TA or your professor to give you a final grade, your TA can chime in and give you an A for effort, which could push your grade up a notch.

You'll Have a Role Model in the Field

If you're passionate about the course matter, your TA could be a major role model and mentor for you, since she knows everything you need to know to succeed in undergrad, knows about all of the extracurricular opportunities to gain experience, and can tell you all about life as a grad student in that field. Plus, if you get close now, you can stay in touch and use her as a contact or reference down the road when you're looking for jobs!

Chapter Checklist

✓ Your RA is the ultimate resource for all things dorm life, plus a great person to turn to if you're feeling homesick or are dealing with roommate issues.

✓ Don't be afraid to tell your RA if you're truly worried about a friend's health or habits! Just know that he may be obligated to report the issue to higher-ups for the sake of everyone's safety.

✓ Becoming an RA has its perks (free room and board is pretty hard to beat), but know that it's not a walk in the park; you have to be ready to help people in tough situations and give it your all.

✓ You might be RA material if you're a great listener and like talking to people, want to help your peers, love to plan events, and don't mind spending time in your room.

✓ Want to get to know your professor or even raise your grade? Always, always, always attend office hours, even if you don't have a specific question! That personal touch is the best way to stand out and show how much you care about the class.

✓ Don't be afraid to disagree with your professor; if you think you deserved more points on a test or essay, bringing it up and discussing the discrepancy could help you get the score you wanted. Just remember that when you disagree, always do it respectfully!

✓ If you're in a larger lecture, your TA is your best resource for personalized advice, answers to specific course-related questions, and advocacy when you need help.

CHAPTER 12

Dating, Relationships, and Hooking Up

Though dating an RA may be off limits, it's about time we focused on all of the relationships you *could* enjoy in college, guilt-free. It should come as no surprise that college opens up a whole wide world to every new collegiette, and with that new world comes a vast new dating pool! Bye-bye, high school boys; hello, campus cuties!

Once you're on campus, you're constantly meeting new people, including tons of new man candy, which inevitably leads to crushes, hook-ups, and relationships. For most students, college is the first time that they have their own space away from their parents, from curfews, and from rules about having members of the opposite sex in their rooms, so things are bound to get a little messy. Is he really into you, or is he just interested in sex? Should you be exclusive? How far should you go? Should you stay with your boyfriend from high school, or play the field? With that awesome collegiate independence comes a ton of real-life relationship decisions, both wonderful and not so wonderful. We've got you covered on how to deal, from dormcest to LDRs (long-distance relationships) and everything in between.

HOOK-UPS

Ah, hook-ups. Rom-coms wouldn't be the same without them, and neither would we. Why? Well, they're entertaining for a reason: They're exciting, because they're all about having fun with someone you're enjoying getting to know, and they lead to the fun little game of "will they or won't they?" when it comes time to finally DTR (define the relationship) and decide if you're dating.

At the same time, hook-ups can actually get really tricky; it's almost impossible to be physical with someone in any capacity without letting feelings get in the way at some point, and you never know which one of you will care more than the other. Plus, when you're just hooking up, you leave the opportunity open for both of you to play the field, which can lead to *Gossip Girl*–style jealousy and drama.

Dormcest

Think long and hard before hooking up with someone who lives in your dorm (a.k.a. dormcest), especially if they're on the same floor as you. Remember that you will probably see him or her every day for the entire school year. Remember that even if it feels good now, it has incredible awkwardness potential—and since you live together, that awkwardness will spread like wildfire to everyone in your dorm.

Whether it's the cute baseball player down the hall, the arty English major one floor up, or the lacrosse-pinnie-sporting, Natty-drinking bro just two doors down, let's face it: Your college dorm is teeming with hotties of every race, creed, and fraternity. Incoming freshmen, get ready: Living with guys is unlike anything you've experienced before. But is it wise to tap into this man candy store knowing there's a risk of bumping into a foiled hook-up every time you walk down the hall to take a shower? Have no fear, collegiettes. Use these fixes for common dormcest pitfalls and you'll be plunging headfirst into intra-dorm relationships before you can say, "Hey, I live on North Campus, too!"

The Pitfall: Mismatched Expectations

It's going to be tempting to jump into romance as soon as you get on campus and realize you have hot guys living next door. Even the girl with the most self-control can have trouble resisting such romantic convenience.

When a gal gets involved with a guy quickly, it can be difficult for both parties involved to know what the expectations for the hook-up are. It's especially important to get these straight with a guy in your dorm—the possibilities of after-hookup awkwardness are that much greater (think a 24/7 walk of shame).

The fix? Spend a couple of weeks just getting to know the guys in your dorm before you take it to a physical level—you'll have a better sense of what they're looking for (and what you're looking for, too). And hey, there is no crime in looking!

The Pitfall: He Sees You at Your Best . . . and Your Not-So-Best

You know the feeling you get when you decide you're interested in a guy: You're consumed by the constant compulsion to touch up your lip gloss, you put your girlfriends on a twenty-four-hour "crush watch" (so you can look like you are NOT trying at all times), and you actually start waking up to shower before class. While we've all succumbed to this Secret Girl Behavior (which we guess is no longer secret), living so close to the guy you're interested in poses a whole new set of challenges. Your same-dorm stud will without a doubt see you at least once in each of the following situations:

1. Walking to the shower in your towel, acne medication (or worse) in hand

2. Coming upstairs to your room at 3 A.M. with a huge pepperoni pizza and no visible friends to share it with

3. Having a loud and embarrassing phone conversation with your mother in the stairwell ("MOM, I told you I do NOT EAT TUNA FISH! STOP SENDING IT TO ME!")

The fix? Well, there really isn't one. Living in close proximity to the boy of your dreams means that he'll get pretty comfortable with your less-than-perfect habits pretty quickly. Learn to crack a joke when he catches you, and at least this way there are no surprises about you in store for him down the road.

The Pitfall: Non-Exclusivity and Shared Living Space

So you've started getting busy on a semi-regular basis with a hottie on your hall. While a late-night rendezvous is much more convenient when only a few yards separate you from your boy du jour, there comes a time when you (or he) may long for a romance outside the dormitory walls. So what do you do when your dormcestual dude catches you coming back with another guy? Or you see him coming back with another girl? Without the promise of exclusivity, these can be quite the sticky situations.

The fix? If you see your guy bringing back another girl, you'll want to quietly and calmly go back to your room, or, better yet, a girlfriend's room. This is not the time for loud, confrontational displays à la *The Real Housewives* reunions. If in the morning you find that you are still disturbed by the thought of your nonexclusive guy with another girl, it may be time to grit your teeth and have "the talk."

If your guy sees you coming back with, well, another guy, be prepared for him to be upset. Again, try to avoid any scenes. You're not technically in the wrong, so leave it up to him to say something later—but know that he may not have anything to say to you at all. Remember that the proximity inherent in dormcest can be a cost as well as a benefit, since there's really no avoiding each other.

The Pitfall: Keeping Dormcest Relationships Fresh

Real, exclusive dormcest relationships can and do work. But they require a bit of an extra effort to reach normalcy. For example, it's not normal to move in with a guy after dating for two weeks, but when you already essentially live together, it can be hard to find that separation you need in the early stages of the relationship. You can go from zero to living together in about a week if you aren't careful. It's easy to get caught up in such a convenient romance, spending Friday nights cuddled up with your guy watching *Friends* reruns while your actual friends are out wondering if you've chosen to study abroad this semester without telling them.

The fix? Make an effort to develop friends and interests that take you out of the dorm—that way, if your romance ends, your life won't! Avoid falling into dead-end routines in your relationship. If every Saturday you and your guy spend the afternoon playing video games with his friends on his hall, eat dinner in your dorm's attached dining hall, and watch movies in your room at night, branch out! Take a walk around campus in the afternoon, try a new restaurant, or go to a party you normally wouldn't attend. It will keep you and your romance fresh!

The Pitfall: Dormcest Doesn't Last Forever

If your dormcestual relationship has an unhappy end, it can be tricky to navigate the post-breakup waters. If you're close to the end of the year, congrats! You won't have to awkwardly cohabit much longer. But if you're not so lucky, seeing your ex-flame at (literally) every turn can really take a toll on your psyche.

The fix? Throw yourself into activities outside the dorm. Do the same things you would do at the end of any relationship, but especially try to put yourself into situations where you won't be spending excessive amounts of time wallowing in your room only to bump into your ex walking to the vending machines to get a soda when you venture out of your room sporting your rattiest sweatpants and mascara tears. If you've really got to do the full-on waterworks, watch-*The-Notebook*-and-eat-a-pint-of-Ben-and-Jerry's routine, consider moving the party to a girlfriend's room in another dorm. Above all, keep your head up, and know that there are infinitely more eligible bachelors outside your dorm than in it.

Now, perhaps you're thinking, With all these pitfalls, why would I ever want to brave dormcest territory? It really can be sweet, all risks aside. Here are the top four perks of dormcest:

1. Your fingers will never freeze in sub-zero January temperatures on your way to see your boy toy.
2. You probably have a lot of the same friends that live in your dorm, thus making social plans together is easy.
3. Whether you're having a good day or bad day, he's always going to be down the hall (or up the stairs).
4. You'll never have to do the walk of shame across campus.

If you dare to dormcest, just keep these pros and cons in mind so you don't get in too deep without taking stock of the situation! Still, of all of the types of hook-ups you may encounter while on campus (which could be none, or could be many), dormcest isn't one of the worst to tangle with (as evidenced by the impressive perks we just mentioned).

Friends with Benefits

What's a really tricky hook-up situation to watch out for? Well, other than the one-night stand and your friend's ex-boyfriend (both of which can open a huge can of worms), the "friends with benefits" (FWB) situation may be one of the most notorious for leading to drama.

FWB is when you and your friend hook up without being romantic (i.e., no candlelit dinners, no sweet pillow talk . . . nothing but maybe playing video games when you aren't playing tonsil hockey). Hollywood would have us believe that although there can be conflict along the way, there's ultimately no going wrong with a FWB situation. Unfortunately, this isn't the case. While FWB relationships can be awesome, they can also be a total disaster. So before you and your best guy friend decide to act on your mutual attraction, here are some things to consider.

Can You Be Honest with Your Emotions?

FWB is typically defined as two people in a platonic relationship who act on a mutual physical attraction. Emotions are not supposed to get involved, and when they do, the situation can become incredibly complicated. If you're not being honest with yourself or him about how you feel, there's a good chance you'll end up heartbroken.

You should never use FWB as a way to secretly try to turn your guy friend into your boyfriend. If you do this, your feelings for him will only get stronger as you continue to hook up. You'll wind up feeling like you're in a relationship with him, and you'll be crushed when he still sees you as only a friend. You also have to be willing to admit if you develop feelings for him in the midst of your friends-with-benefitting.

If you're honest with yourselves and with each other, things can work out, but the key is to remember that there's a difference between sex and love, and FWB is about hooking up. If you don't think that you can be honest about those lines getting blurred, you should probably avoid starting an FWB relationship.

Are You the Jealous Type?

Another important thing to think about before kicking your friendship into overdrive is whether or not you tend to become territorial over someone you're hooking up with. FWB relationships aren't real relationships; they're more a series of one-night stands. This means that they also tend not to be monogamous.

If you know you're the type of person who can't handle hooking up with someone who is also consistently hooking up with other people, you should steer clear of a FWB relationship. The nature of FWB is that the relationship isn't going to turn into anything more in the future. This means that if your guy friend is pursuing other girls while he's still hooking up with you, you have to be okay with it. You need to be able to accept the fact that his going out on dates with another girl is not equal to him cheating on you.

Have You Established Rules?

A good method of keeping the lines of your FWB relationship clearly drawn is establishing ground rules before you get involved. Obviously, if your first hook-up happens when you're drunk, this may not be possible. But even if that's the case, you can still establish rules before you two get into the pattern of hooking up regularly.

FWB rules can help you make sure that your guy friend doesn't start to seem like he's your boyfriend (or, you know, your fiancé-in-training, since you know that'll cross your mind eventually; can you say, secret Pinterest wedding board?). If you aren't careful, these thoughts may be swirling around in your head before you know it, distracting you from the fabulous should-be simplicity of the FWB situation you had on your hands.

- **No new friend or family introductions:** If he's already part of your friend group, this can't be avoided, but you should avoid integrating him more into your daily routine. Seeing him meet and get along with your friends and family is going to make you much more likely to develop deeper feelings for him.
- **No gifts:** Even if you two have exchanged presents in the past, gift-giving between FWB can be a very tricky business. Getting a gift from someone you're hooking up with can push the relationship dangerously close to dating. It's also incredibly difficult for both people to not overanalyze gifts in this situation.
- **No sleepovers:** Cuddling and sleeping over after hooking up with someone can become very emotional and intimate. If you two are constantly having sleepovers after hooking up, one of you is going to start feeling confused about what the status of your relationship is.
- **Full disclosure:** If you two are both going to be hooking up with other people during your FWB relationships, you have to decide if you're going to tell each other when it happens. Safe sex is an incredibly important aspect of FWB, and if you're not going to feel comfortable not knowing when he's been with someone else, you need to tell him that before you two get involved.

These rules are only possible suggestions. Every FWB relationship is different, so it's up to you to decide what you do and don't want to talk about beforehand.

Are You Willing to Risk Losing His Friendship?
The most important thing to consider before starting a FWB relationship is whether or not you're willing to risk losing his

friendship. FWB has the potential to ruin a really great friendship if things don't go well.

If one of you develops romantic feelings for the other during the relationship, it's incredibly difficult to go back to just the friendship you once had. The person who has feelings will end up hurt, the person who doesn't will end up feeling awkward, and your old dynamic will disappear.

There are both pros and cons to FWB relationships. So if you've considered all the outcomes and it still seems worth it to you, then give it a try!

Hook-ups are only half of the romantic relationships in college—the other half being actual relationships, and of course the fabulous #singleladies life—but they sure make for a heck of a lot of great stories (and some not-so-great stories, if you find yourself in an FWB or dormcest situation that's gone south). Still, the journey is the reward, collegiettes!

DATING

If you do manage to turn a hook-up into a full-fledged relationship (or, by some miracle, manage to find that elusive college guy who likes to go on dates off campus and gets to know you that way—yay you!), you'll find that the rules of dating are entirely different than the rules of casual flings. New to the college dating scene? We've got you covered!

When you're a freshman girl, eligible cuties seem to be everywhere. And guess what? They're all looking at *you*. The attention can be fun, but when it comes down to it, the dating game in college is one that you'll learn a lot about as time goes on—you might not be a pro right off the bat. To get you started, we've put together a list of the dos and don'ts of college dating. Who, you ask, knew there was such a science behind college guys, anyway? Aren't they just a bunch of sex-hungry dudes? Well, maybe, but there might be a little bit more to it. Here are the guidelines of how to deal with the ones who are, and the ones who aren't.

Do Make Friends with the Guys on Your Floor

These guys will be super fun to hang out with once they get to know each other well, and you'll be the cool girl who can get in on that action when you need a break from girl drama. On top of it, you might really connect with one of them (though be sure to check out our advice on dormcest earlier in this chapter if you do!).

Don't Write Anybody Off Too Soon

Just because he's sitting alone and doesn't speak to anyone in the class doesn't mean he's a total lunatic. If you're interested, all it takes is a slow pack-up-and-hang-back after class to initiate conversation.

Do Go Out to Meet People

Find out where the hot spots are each night of the week(end), and make sure to show up every once in a while. As a new student, you'll get a feel for student life and get exposed to every kind of guy—frat boys, athletes, pre-meds, business students, and artsy guys, too.

Don't Stay in Talking to Your High School Boyfriend Every Night

If you've broken up, there was a reason, and now is the time to move on. Your freshman year is meant for new beginnings, not dwelling on old relationships. If you broke up, phone calls between Texas and Massachusetts won't bring you back together—it'll only keep you from meeting new people that are just beyond your dorm room door. If you're still together and trying to make an LDR work, you still should make time to hang with friends and meet new people rather than locking yourself inside every night to Skype your guy. It's not social, and it's not great for your happiness on campus, either!

Five-Question Test

Maybe you're a New England sweetheart and he's a California surfer dude, maybe he's a debonair European and you're heading back to the States after a semester of studying abroad, or maybe you're high school sweethearts heading off to college for the first time. Either way, you're now weighing the possibility of doing a long-distance relationship for at least the duration of the summer or semester. While a couple of months may not seem like the end of the world, it's hard to imagine not being able to call your boy up and suggest an impromptu movie night whenever you want. Long-distance relationships, no matter the time (and miles) spent apart, are challenging. Ask yourself these five questions when deciding whether going long-distance is the answer.

- How long will the separation last?
- How busy will you be this summer/semester?
- How often will you be able to talk to him, and will you get to see each other in person at all?
- Will you be exclusive or not exclusive?
- Do you trust him?

These can be difficult and awkward questions to ask, but they'll save you a lot of heartache (not to mention fights) later on.

Do Start Off Slowly If You're Not Used to Dating or Just Got Out of a Relationship

Study-hall or dining-hall dates count, too! As casual as these settings are, it can be a great place to get to know a guy or meet someone new. Take it easy if you're just getting your feet wet with the whole dating game, and don't feel a need to rush into anything intense.

Don't Go Out Every Single Night

A little mystery never hurt anyone . . . and it'll do wonders for your grades, too. Show face as often as you can without being that girl whom everyone expects to run into.

Do Look Around Your Classes for Guys

If he's showing up for class at all, then you know he's got something going for him. And hey, maybe he's even smart and organized enough for you to make him your study buddy. Study dates are pretty much the best dates most college girls can hope for within the first month or so of school (news flash: college guys are usually cheap).

Don't Make Him Think You're Interested If You're Not Just Because You Want the Perks

It's not fair to the guy if you're just not that into him but you keep him around because he's, like, obsessed with you. The puppy-dog thing will get old after a while, leaving him feeling stupid and angry and you feeling unfulfilled, annoyed, and guilty—not to mention that other guys you might actually become interested in will get the wrong idea.

Do Engage in a Random Hook-Up (Safely) If You Want To

They're part of the college lifestyle, and you can choose if you want to engage in them or not (certainly, you can avoid making out with the guy you've been dancing with all night if you're just not that into it). It's up to you to decide if that's your style, but know that it happens and it doesn't have to be scandalous or "slutty"—but just, in fact, kind of fun. As long as you're not going crazy by swapping saliva with every guy you lay eyes on, random hook-ups can be fun and can lead to date parties, formals, and maybe even a real date! If nothing else, at least you can get an exciting night or two out of them—just make sure to stay safe and keep your friends posted on your whereabouts.

Don't Count on Random Hook-Ups Turning Into Anything Serious

Most of the time, dance-floor makeouts (DFMOs) start and finish on the dance floor and only go as far as a phone number swap. Take these experiences for what they are, and don't think he's fallen in love with you simply because he's been attached to your mouth all night.

Do Accept Invitations and Initiations from Older Guys

Attention from upperclassmen is surely a plus in any freshman's book because these guys are seasoned. They know what's up in this whole college world, and it can be quite nice to have a hot, older guy show you the ropes—he'll let you know what parties are happening, bring you to date events, and introduce you to his friends. That said, don't feel the need to hook up with him purely because he's "older and wiser," because he may just turn out to be pretty stupid.

Don't Get Too Attached to Said Upperclassman

He's graduating sooner than you are, and he knows it. Upperclassmen usually aren't in it for the long haul when they seek out a freshman girl that they'd like to hook up with. Just because he's lent you a bunch of attention one night doesn't mean you should assume that he'll be chasing after you for the rest of the semester.

Don't Feel Pressured to Have Sex

No, we can't be certain that what all guys are looking for is sex, but that's definitely a part of college hook-ups. He might want it and he might even ask for it, but if you're uncomfortable, you don't have to give it to him. Know your boundaries and ask him—whether you know him well or not—to respect your boundaries; if he doesn't, walk away.

Do Avoid Those Guys Who Hook Up with Your Entire Group of Friends

There are always the guys who have no qualms about coming in between a group of girlfriends just to get some action. He has no problem with hooking up with each one of your friends by jumping from one to the next. He might have no idea that what he's doing is hurting your relationships with your friends, but it's up to you and your friends to stop him by cutting him out of the equation.

Do Be Open to Going on Dates with Anyone

That is, of course, presuming that dates aren't obsolete anymore. While a lot of guys don't even have the courtesy to take a girl out for dinner—or even coffee?!—there are some who like to kick it old school and go for the dinner and a movie. If you're looking for companionship of any kind, there's no reason to refuse a casual invitation to lunch or dinner.

Don't Expect Him to Take You Out to Fancy Meals All the Time

But at the same time, know that college culture is changing, and going out on the "dates" we see happening in movies or the ones we hear about from our parents simply doesn't happen anymore, for the most part. These guys are most likely on a budget, so fancy dinner dates aren't always an option. There's nothing wrong with a nice fro-yo in the quad, though!

Don't Count on Finding a Boyfriend Right Away

Keep in mind that though you see a lot of hotties on a regular basis, most of them aren't right for you. It's about finding the right one who's interested in having the same type of relationship that you are, no matter what type that may be. Also, be wary of becoming BF/GF with someone on day one of orientation. Do some exploring before you settle on one guy to get hot and heavy with right away.

Do Start a Relationship If You Find Someone Special

Maybe you'll find him on day one of classes, or maybe it'll take until senior year for you to realize that the guy you've been friends with all along suddenly seems like he's ready to take the plunge with you. If it feels right, don't hold back, and find a way to make it work.

Do Know That People Move On Quickly in College

Hook-ups last for any length of time—you can be attached to one particular guy for several months and it can still be considered "hooking up." Go figure. At any rate, don't be surprised if a guy has eyes for you on Thursday and then you spot him chatting up another girl on Saturday. Don't get jealous or crazy and be that girl who slaps him in the middle of the party. Instead, try to figure out what he's interested in before you hook up with him so you know what to expect from him after the fact.

Don't Hold Back If You Want Something More Out of a Hook-Up

If you silence yourself, you'll only end up unhappy and wasting your time. If your relationship started out as a random hook-up, he may not be taking it as seriously as you wished he would. If your feelings intensify and you want to take it to the next level, let him know and don't make him guess. If you're afraid of scaring him off, leave your feelings on the table and the situation open-ended. This is his relationship, too, and you don't want to monopolize it, so ask him what it is that he wants out of it. Chances are that otherwise he won't just guess that you want to be treated to romantic dinners, and you'll just end up getting frustrated and angry.

Do Try to Meet Guys Without a Gaggle of Girls Surrounding You

While girls' night out is always one of the best nights of the week, do try to distance yourself from your pack of besties for a little bit each night. No guy wants to approach you if your six best friends are by your side eyeing him with those girly, judgmental glares.

Don't Get Left Places Alone or Go Home with a Guy You Don't Know

Having made out with him all night doesn't make him any more familiar. If you do manage to separate from your girlfriends for a few minutes, keep in touch with them to make sure they're not leaving the club/bar/party without you. It's risky to leave with a guy you've just met—especially if one of his friends who "didn't drink tonight" is driving—even if he seems genuine. Exchange numbers instead, and stay with your girlfriends.

College will open doors for you in the way of the dating scene, but it always helps to take things slowly and be wary. Stay grounded and always question people's intentions, while making sure that your own are as clear as crystal. Your future boyfriend is out there somewhere, whether he's sitting next to you in class or isn't even enrolled at your school. And you'll find him, too . . . you just may have to kiss a few frogs and have a lot of single-girl fun first.

SEX

It's easy enough to talk about all of the excitement of the dating pool of college, but whether you've already dated someone or have been a single lady (and loving it) for a long time now, that doesn't mean that you're necessarily experienced sexually, and you don't have to be! Most collegiettes arrive on campus as virgins, and many leave it four years later as virgins, too.

What to Expect from Your First Time

If you've never had sex, you may be anxious about your first time. That's why it's important to choose a partner you feel comfortable and open with and to take things slowly. Foreplay of any kind can help you ease in and relax. Your first time may or may not hurt, depending on a variety of factors, and you shouldn't necessarily expect to orgasm. What's important is that you feel ready and safe, and keep in mind that feeling anxiety about your first time is totally normal!

Seven Reasons Why You've Never Had a Boyfriend (and Why That's Totally Okay!)

Ever felt like you woke up one day and every girl you knew had a boyfriend? Your best friend does, your frenemy does, and even that weird girl in your chem lab seems to be cuddling up with some cutie in between classes. What gives? To all the collegiettes out there who feel perpetually single, don't worry! There are plenty of reasons why you've never had a boyfriend, and there are an infinite number of reasons why it's totally okay that you haven't.

1.   You've been focusing on your studies and extracurricular activities.
2.   You rush to your 8 A.M. history class, and then you go to three more classes, a working lunch for a group project,

two club meetings, a quick trip to the gym, your on-campus job, a 7 P.M. bio review, and then the library to do homework. By the end of the day, you're exhausted and just want to head to bed. Where in your schedule would there be time to keep up with a boyfriend?

3. You're not a huge fan of your current dating pool.

4. Let's face it: Guys can be immature, annoying, rude, hard to read (or too easy to read), and every other problematic adjective in between. These all can be unappealing reasons to date for many collegiettes, and it could be why you're having trouble finding someone to call your beau. Guys do eventually change (sometimes), so if the guys in your class year or at your college just aren't cutting it for you, remember that there's always hope for the future!

5. You just don't want a boyfriend.

6. Some collegiettes get pressured into finding a boyfriend since it can seem like everyone around you has one or is looking, but you definitely shouldn't seek out a BF unless you actually want to have one. Sometimes dealing with the drama just doesn't feel worth your time, so don't force it!

7. Every college movie shows young adults trying to "find themselves" in some way or another, and while *Accepted* might not be the most accurate depiction of college life, the overall theme rings true: College students are still figuring things out. This can definitely include your likes, dislikes, and everything in between, and it also could be why you may not have had a boyfriend.

Just because you've never had a boyfriend doesn't mean there's something wrong with you! College is about self-discovery and deciding what you want for yourself. Your priorities might not include a boyfriend, and that's perfectly fine. In addition, not wanting a boyfriend doesn't make you weird; it makes you smart because you're focusing on what's best for you. Think about the balance you want in your life. Your happiness should come first!

If we were to believe everything we saw in movies, we would think that virginity was worse than the bubonic plague. Thanks to sex-centered teen flicks like *Mean Girls, American Pie, The To Do List*, and more, many of us collegiettes have grown up thinking of virginity as some backwards, juvenile label you need to shed before moving on to the mature world that is the college campus (to which we have to say: There's so much wrong with that sentence). We find some cute guy or girl at a party, we lose our virginity, and voilà! We become women. Problem solved, right?

The reality? Tons of collegiettes, not just freshmen, are still carrying their V-cards—and there's absolutely nothing wrong with that. Still, some collegiettes can't help but worry about the way it'll affect their love lives (and about what guys think of girls who are still virgins). In truth, some virgins do struggle in the hypersexual college hook-up scene (as if we really need to tack that onto our list of freshman-year worries about roommates, picking classes, and whether our minifridges will really keep our Ben & Jerry's pints icy fresh). That said, you should always feel comfortable doing as much or as little as you want to, and you should never let anyone pressure you into moving faster than you're prepared to move.

So, how's a collegiette supposed to know when the time is really right? The key is knowing how to tell when *you* are ready. Whether you're a virgin or are contemplating having sex with a new partner, first times can be nerve-racking. There are many factors to consider, both emotional and physical.

When Is the Right Time to Have Sex in a Relationship?

Some girls wait until marriage, some wait a few months, and some wait just a few dates. There's no recommended timeline—the right time to have sex is when you and your partner feel ready. For some people, that's when they stop thinking about it or worrying about it; they don't doubt the other person's intentions and trust that they're on the same page. For others, it takes a bit longer to get comfortable, and they decide to wait until they're certain they're in love. That's a great way to avoid any regrets down the road!

Furthermore, consider your mental health. Are you depressed, overly stressed, or anxious? Take a step back. It's natural to seek out sex when we're looking for emotional comfort, but it's not the greatest choice, since if it's a new development for you, it will just become one more potential stressor in your life. Being in a relatively good mental headspace isn't required for sex, but trying to be intimate when you're feeling so vulnerable usually hurts rather than helps the situation.

Sex is a two-way street, so your partner should be ready, too. Can the both of you trust each other? Do you feel comfortable enough having potentially awkward conversations (about contraception, what you do and don't like sexually, etc.)? Are you both mature enough to handle the consequences, good and bad, of sex? This isn't an exhaustive list by any means, but you should make sure you know your limits and the other person's limits before having sex.

Regardless of when you decide is the right time, your and your partner's opinions are the only ones that count. There can be pressure to have sex in college, but that shouldn't influence your decision.

Who to Tell If You've Had Sex

Sex is an incredibly personal decision and it's up to you how widely (or not) you want to broadcast that choice. However, it is important that you be honest with your doctor about your sexual activity. She will not be judgmental and is only looking out for your health! Whether you want to share these details with anyone beyond your doctor—such as your mom, your friends, or your roommate—is up to you.

Five Conversations You Need to Have Before Having Sex

Not everything about sex is actually sexy. Some conversations with a new partner can be awkward to bring up, but if you're going to be intimate with someone, you need to be able to talk openly. Before jumping in the sack with your crush, you should discuss these important topics.

Define Your Expectations

Make sure you and your partner know exactly what adding sex to the relationship will mean for you and what your expectations for it are. If having sex means you're in love with this person and this is your way of expressing it, make sure your partner knows that. If it's just sex and you aren't looking for a commitment from it, be sure to make that clear.

Talk about Getting Tested

Although this isn't the sexiest conversation, it's definitely an important one to have. Ask your partner if he or she has gotten tested in the last six months and if he or she might have picked up any STD or STIs since then. It's better to be safe than sorry, so don't be afraid to bring it up.

Talk about Contraception

On the same note, unless you're down to having this guy's baby or want to risk getting an STD or STI, you need to discuss what form of contraception you will be using. Let him know if you are on the pill or if there's another form of birth control that you use. Discuss using condoms and make sure you both have them.

DTR: Are You Exclusive?

You don't want to think you're exclusive and then hear around campus that your partner was with someone else—or vice versa, since thinking you're not exclusive when your partner thought otherwise can be messy, too.

Define Your Boundaries

Some people like chocolate ice cream and some like vanilla. Your partner may be into or ready for some things that you aren't ready for. It's also common that your definition of sex is different than your partner's. That's why it's important to discuss the things you and your partner are willing to do so you aren't taken by surprise by something you may not be comfortable with.

Take control of your sexual health and make sure you're communicating with your partner. Sometimes we rush into things when we're swooning over our crush, but it's important to keep yourself safe. Remember to discuss these topics before taking the next step!

Will Sex Improve My Relationship?

Maybe, maybe not. Regardless of whether or not it might, that's not a good reason to have sex with someone. There are a lot of bad reasons to have sex: pressure (from both your partner and your peers), a desire to "get it over with," feeling that you have to, and because you think sex will fix your relationship—just to name a few. But there are a TON of great reasons, too! Sex can be fun, intense, and passionate! A lot of girls do it for the emotional aspect. There isn't a "best" reason to have sex. And sex also doesn't have to be some intense act of love if you and your partner don't want it to be.

Sex isn't simple—you have to make smart choices and know yourself well enough to recognize when you're ready and when you aren't. But once you feel like you're ready, it can be pretty awesome!

At the end of the day, there's a lot to consider when it comes to the college dating and hook-up scenes: You have to know what you're looking for, what you're comfortable with doing, whom you trust, how to balance your time, and how to find someone who's willing to make all of that work with you. Fortunately, there are plenty of fish in the sea that is your college campus, so we have a feeling you can find the lucky guy whenever you're ready!

Wellness Check-In: Five Signs You're in a Healthy Relationship

If you do decide that a relationship is the way to go—whether it's a consistent hook-up or a bona fide boyfriend/girlfriend situation—make sure that it's a healthy relationship before you fall head over heels for him. How can you tell, though, when you get the warm fuzzies whenever he's around? That can make it hard to tell whether it's truly amazing or whether the butterflies in your stomach are clouding your judgment. You'll know you're in a healthy situation if:

You Can Be Honest with Him

You should always feel like you're being yourself (and not afraid of showing it) whenever you're around your guy, if your relationship is a healthy one. Sure, it's natural to not give everything away right off the bat; after all, you might scare him off if you reveal your obsessive love of cats or your penchant for collecting antique dolls on day one. After a little while, though, you should feel that you can share these things without fear of judgment or criticism. Plus, it's crucial that you feel that you can talk to him about anything that's bothering you, be it in your relationship or outside of it (for instance, the fact that you want to see him more during the daytime or that you're upset about your low essay grade should both be up for discussion, and he should be supportive of you in both conversations!).

You Can Be Honest with Your Friends

It's incredibly important that you can be honest with your guy, but it's equally important that you can open up to your girlfriends, too. You should be able to tell them how you're feeling about your relationship, sharing the highs and the lows and seeking their advice along the way. If for some reason you feel embarrassed or ashamed to tell your friends what's going on, that could be a sign that something's not right in your relationship, whether it's poor communication, a lack of intimacy, an issue with his personality, a conflict between him and your friends, verbal abuse, or worse. If you aren't excited or willing to share important details with your friends or you feel that you have to tell white lies to get your friends to like your guy, there's probably major trouble in paradise.

You Trust Each Other

Every healthy relationship is built on a foundation of trust, so don't let yourself end up in a relationship without that fundamental feature. If he doesn't trust you, you'll feel guilty or self-conscious about things you should never question, such as chatting with a male friend in class or keeping in touch with your ex-boyfriend (which should be okay, provided it's now a completely platonic relationship). If you don't trust him, you'll constantly feel suspicious and guarded, which only brings conflict to the relationship. If one of you is afraid of the other cheating (or one of you already has cheated), it can be nearly impossible to make the relationship the supportive, healthy, loving one it should be.

You Feel Safe Physically

It seems obvious, but it's important to remind yourself: You should always feel safe physically whenever you're around your boyfriend or hook-up, no matter what your level of commitment. If he gets angry and you're worried that he might hurt you, you shouldn't be with him. If you're physically intimate and he pushes you to go further than you want to with him, you shouldn't be with him, and you definitely shouldn't feel pressured to oblige him. At the end of the day, the person who should matter most to you in the relationship is you, and that means you have to keep yourself safe—even if it means breaking things off. If you're in a healthy relationship, you'll know that your body is your own, even if you're choosing to share it with your guy.

You're Happier When You're with Him, but You're Happy When You're Not, Too

The mark of the best relationships is the happiness you feel when you're together—the kind of happiness that doesn't fade the second that you separate, be it for winter break, for a long weekend, or even for class. You should feel over-the-moon happy when you get to be with your guy, but when you take a break for girls' night out or spend the day studying with friends, you should feel happy, well-adjusted, and totally functional, not down in the dumps because you're aren't with your hook-up buddy. If you find yourself unable to be apart without thinking of him constantly, complaining that you're not together, isolating yourself, or counting the minutes until your reunion, then you're definitely too attached for your relationship to be healthy.

Healthy relationships are happy relationships, and they're the only kind you should look for in college! Whether you're already head over heels or just starting to hook up, you'll want to watch out for signs that things are going south (and head them off before they do). You deserve only the best, and that means the best feelings, too. The last thing you want is to look back at college and wonder why you wasted your time with people who weren't good for you!

Chapter Checklist

✓ Dormcest can be tempting, given proximity and convenience, but remember that a romantic interaction today could make for an awkward run-in tomorrow. If you live near each other, you'll have to learn to deal with each other, so don't get in over your head!

✓ A FWB situation only works if both of you are on the same page about what you want. If one of you falls for the other and feelings aren't returned, your friendship could fall to pieces. Be honest with each other!

✓ If you're staying in a long-distance relationship, don't forget to make time to meet new people and hang with friends. Spending all of your time Skyping your beau will only narrow your social circle at school, making it harder to be happy and feel independent.

✓ Don't feel pressured to have sex! Even when it seems like everyone on campus has experience (and expects the same of you), that's not true; everyone moves at his or her own pace. You won't enjoy it unless you're 100 percent ready, so why rush?

✓ If you do choose to have sex, be safe and make sure that you trust your partner to help you feel comfortable.

✓ You'll know if you're in a healthy relationship when you can be honest, feel safe, trust your partner, and be happy even if he isn't there.

CHAPTER 13

Unhealthy Relationships

It's so important to foster healthy relationships in college, whether they're with your brand-new boy toy, your roomie, or the besties who've become your go-to wingwomen. If you don't, you'll find yourself even more stressed than necessary, with no one to support you when you're dealing with difficult deadlines, homesickness, or breakups that require Ben & Jerry's.

It may seem like a no-brainer to find BFFs and boyfriends who actually care about you (and treat you the way you deserve to be treated), but if you're not careful, you could fall into superficial friendships or relationships out of convenience (hello, hallmates!) and miss the signs of a union gone awry.

ROTTEN ROMANTIC RELATIONSHIPS

Taylor Swift said it best with "I Knew You Were Trouble," we collegiettes have a sixth sense for sniffing out bad boys. However, the unwashed, tatted up, leather-clad guy on the motorcycle isn't the only troublemaker you should steer clear of (although anyone who reminds you of Russell Brand in any way should probably be given a wide berth). We're talking about the guys who aren't quite so obvious about their womanizing, the sensitive artists, and the quarterback types who, underneath their shiny, nice-guy exteriors, just might be Charlie Sheens in training. So how can you really tell if he's a rotten egg? Be on the lookout for these seven sure signs he's a heartbreaker.

He's a Last-Minute, Late-Night Caller

You know that your guy has free time during the week—last we checked, watching hockey wasn't an academic requirement—but he waits until 10 P.M. on a Friday night to ask you to hang out. At first you're flattered and pumped to get to spend time with him. It isn't until the next weekend when it happens all over again that you think to yourself, "Why didn't he make plans with me earlier?" It's a red flag if he needs beer goggles or liquid courage to hang out with you, and, just as bad, it could mean that he has some other ladies on the side. Needless to say, if you're not number one on his list of ladies—or if he has a list of ladies at all, for that matter—he isn't worth your time.

He Goes MIA

With cell phones, Facebook, Twitter, and Snapchat, there's hardly any way a college kid could slip off the radar. Yet, somehow, that troublemaker of a guy you've been texting has successfully managed to go missing. He doesn't text, he doesn't call, and he doesn't answer any of your messages (of which there hopefully weren't very many). Then, days or weeks later, he's back, asking you to hang out. No explanation, no excuses—or just incredibly lame ones. What gives? It probably means he's playing the field and you're his backup option, which is definitely not okay (and not conducive to a healthy relationship). Don't let yourself be the last to know when the signs are already loud and clear!

He Badmouths All of His Exes

There are two simple explanations behind your boy-toy's trash-talking: first, that he's perfect. Of course all of his last relationship's problems were his ex's fault, not his, because he's infallible. Case closed. The other (and more likely) explanation is that he's self-righteous, he's critical, and he would rather take a punch than a rejection.

No one likes listening to a whiner, and why hang around a guy who only focuses on the negatives? Chances are he'd say similar things about you if you were to date and break up, and you definitely don't want to be the next ex whose dirty laundry he airs in public.

He Disses Your Friends

The golden rule of girl code: friends over flirts, always. It's one thing if he's disrespecting girls whom he's chosen to be with—the insecurity and blabber-mouthing are never good signs, but he might regret dating those girls for legitimate reasons. It's entirely another if he's disrespecting girls that you've chosen to be with: your BFFs.

You chose your best friends for a reason. Whether they're witty, friendly, or wonderful wingwomen, they've earned your stamp of approval. If a guy says your friends aren't worth your time, he's not just questioning them; he's also questioning your judgment. Definitely not okay.

Seven Things You Should Never Have to Settle For
1. Any form of abuse
2. Constant fighting
3. Lack of attention from your partner
4. Addictive habits
5. Your SO is in lust, not love
6. No longer feeling special
7. Pressure to change

He Guards His Phone with His Life

It's the most obvious sign in the trouble-spotting handbook: If a guy is secretive about or protective of his phone, he probably has something to hide. Chances are, whatever he's hiding isn't something that Prince Charming would approve of.

If your guy is ignoring phone calls and texts, paranoid about letting you scroll through his pictures, and just acting sketchy in general, he probably has a skeleton in his closet. Or, more likely, another girl.

He Immediately Gives You Pet Names

Honey. Baby. Sweetie. If it sounds sugary, cute, and fitting for a fluffy new puppy, it's a pet name. You may be flattered at first, but remind yourself how impersonal those nicknames are. The important thing to remember is that, though it may be an adorable name, it isn't your name. Who's to say he isn't calling other girls by the same one? In the worst cases, it can be a way to avoid calling one girl by another girl's name by accident. Yikes.

He's Only Got Guy Friends

While it's generally much easier to date a guy who isn't attached at the hip to his best girl friend—none of us envy Cameron Diaz in *My Best Friend's Wedding* competing with best friend and all-around awesome lady Julia Roberts—it's not promising when you're dating a guy who has no girl friends at all.

A guy without any lady friends probably isn't getting good dating advice, might not give women the respect they deserve, and almost definitely won't be willing to sit through *The Notebook* with you when you're sick. Cross him off the list.

Whether you're looking for an FWB or the love of your life, you want to steer clear of the players of the world. When you can tell that he's trouble, get out of his way! There are plenty of other guys on campus who will mean it when they say that they want to get to know you, and we'd bet big bucks that they'd give anything for you to give them the chance to do it.

If you do find yourself in a relationship with a bad boy or someone who just isn't good for you (or ready for a relationship in general), you have to be careful not to get in too deep and to make your exit before his treatment of you goes from bad to worse.

Very Early Warning Signs of Abuse

Some of the earliest signs of abuse can include: blaming his negative feelings and bad luck on someone else; caring so much about himself that he becomes insensitive to the feelings and rights of others; believing that he deserves special treatment from others; pointing out why he's smarter or better than others; creating large issues out of small problems; boosting his own ego by making witty comments about something he doesn't agree with; exaggerating or telling lies about his own qualities or experiences to boost his self-confidence; getting (or even just looking) upset if you talk to or look at another guy; wanting you so much that he doesn't care about whether you are comfortable or not.

FRENEMIES

While you should always be on the lookout for bad boys who are also bad eggs, beware one of the worst toxic relationships on campus: the frenemy friendship. Think you're immune to *Mean Girls*–style backstabbing besties? We hope you are, too! But just in case, it's good to watch out for less-than-wonderful friends like these.

We've all heard it: *"You're going to eat all of that?" "Oh, that's my shirt? It looks so different on you." "You just started studying for the history exam? I started three weeks ago." "I just love your healthy curves!" "I mean, I don't think he's attractive, but I guess you like guys like that."* Women come across these types of friendships throughout their lives: In preschool, it's the girl who befriends you just so she can play with your brand-new Malibu Barbie. In middle school, she slips love letters in your crush's locker. In high school, she was secretly pleased when you didn't get into the college of your dreams. In college, these frenemies still exist. They compete to see who can get more attention from guys, who scores higher grades on exams, and whose butt looks cuter in the latest skinny jeans from Urban.

If you think one of your friends might be crossing into frenemy territory, evaluate the situation: Was this a one-time thing, or has this person let you down on numerous occasions? Have you been communicating clearly? How will a friend breakup affect your mutual friends? If your frenemy is bringing you down Regina George–style, you don't deserve it. It's time to get rid of her. Breaking it off with a close friend is just as difficult as ending a relationship with a significant other, but sometimes it has to be done.

TOXIC FRIENDSHIPS

Although frenemies are sometimes the easiest bad friends to identify (because it's hard to let a cutting, two-faced compliment slide without noticing how awful the person who said it made you feel), they certainly aren't the only type you'll encounter as a collegiette on campus.

Your friends are your rock; you can always count on them for a good laugh or a shoulder to cry on. You'd be lost without them, right? Well, not necessarily. Your friendships could actually be hurting you and your health much more than you might think. Some friends might be unhappy or unhealthy themselves, but you shouldn't be afraid to move on from friends who are just plain bad news for your health.

Her Unhealthy Habits Influence You
The Situation
You probably have a lot in common with your friends; that's why you're friends in the first place! Even if you don't like some of the things a friend does, spending time with her might make her other

habits rub off on you. This can be a great thing, an opportunity to grow and evolve—unless her habits have the potential to hurt you.

Drinking or eating to excess, spending too much money, smoking, frequently neglecting assignments in favor of Netflix, or circulating negative thoughts about body image are all bad habits that can rub off from friends.

Why It Happens

We're strong, ambitious collegiettes, and we (usually) know how to make the right decisions! So why are we so easily influenced by our friends' habits? The truth is, a lot of these bad habits seem fun at first glance, and that's why we're willing to try them.

This makes a lot of sense, especially since we often want to look back on our college years as the most fun time of our lives. For instance, if you're feeling swamped with homework, it can be tempting to follow your party-loving friend and join her for nights out on the town instead of buckling down and completing yet another reading assignment.

As for much less seemingly fun bad habits, such as a friend's unhealthy eating patterns, the influence can stem from having similar tendencies to start with. In this situation, your friend would just bring out these tendencies in you rather than create them.

How to Deal

So your friend encourages you to engage in activities that make you uncomfortable or put you at risk. What should you do? Just limit your time together, plain and simple. Or you can choose to see her in a group rather than one-on-one, since you'll feel much less peer pressure when you're surrounded by others who might behave differently than she does.

You Compare Yourself to Her

The Situation

If a friend of yours has low self-esteem and repeatedly lists her perceived faults and failings, you might become more likely to see those same faults in yourself by comparison. Conversely, if your friend is very confident and seems perfect to you, you might feel unworthy compared to her.

Why It Happens

Don't worry if you have a tendency to compare yourself to others, because comparing ourselves to our friends is natural. Just make sure you aren't doing it to excess. If your fit friend inspires you to go to the gym or your book-smart friend motivates you to study an extra hour, by all means, go ahead! If, however, those inspirations and motivations feel more like guilt trips or compensations, then that's a sign you're not comparing yourself in a healthy way.

How to Deal

Avoid negative self-talk within your group of friends by refusing to participate. If your besties are all chatting about how they hate their thighs or how they wish they hadn't eaten that last piece of cake or that they think no boys will ever like them, remind yourself that those trains of thought only lead to even more negative headspaces. Change the topic or say that you don't want to talk like that. If it doesn't work and the negativity continues, and your mood and self-confidence start slumping as a result, it might be time to move on to new friends.

If you have the opposite problem, that is, envying an apparently flawless friend, remember that the grass is always greener on the other side, and it's probably not all sunshine and roses over there! Everyone has insecurities and flaws, so know that your bestie isn't any more perfect than you are.

Bottom line: as hard as it may be, try to maintain a positive and realistic outlook on yourself. Comparing yourself to your friends, whether they're insecure or perfectly confident, has a good chance of bringing you down—unless you use it as healthy motivation.

She Pressures You Into Certain Behaviors

The Situation

Usually our friends have our backs, but sometimes a so-called friend will make us feel obliged to engage in something we don't want to do.

Peer pressure is pervasive in middle and high school, but it most definitely doesn't stop happening in college. Your friends might pressure you to drink, use drugs, or hook up with people for all the wrong reasons.

Why It Happens

You may know your personal limits, but when a friend you trust is egging you on, it can become incredibly difficult to exercise self-control and say no. No one expects you to be Superwoman! Still, not saying "no" to peer pressures like these can lead to dangerous situations.

How to Deal

If one of your friends has a tendency to pressure you into doing things you're uncomfortable with, try seeing her in a group or planning ahead to hang out in a "safe zone," like a restaurant, a movie theater, or the dining hall.

However, if you think your friend's behavior is endangering her health as well as yours, you should let her know that you're worried. Be direct, don't accuse her of anything, and make it clear that you really care about her and her well-being.

Expect that the conversation might not go as planned. If she gets hostile or if things still don't change in your friendship, it's time to go your separate ways.

She Takes More Than She Gives

The Situation

A friendship is an exchange; both of you should be giving as much as you take. If your friend expects more from you than you can possibly give her and gives very little in return, it can become a problem.

A one-sided relationship where you're always on the giving side can really take its toll on your health. You'll probably feel that you're being taken advantage of, and it can majorly mess with your mood and stress levels. When you're dealing with your own drama, the last thing you need is for a "friend" to dump all of hers on you nightly, asking you to make it all better but doing nothing to help you with your own dilemmas.

How to Deal

It's up to you to decide whether the relationship is worth keeping. Indeed, there is a difference between a friend who doesn't give back once or twice and a friend who fails you time and time again. Nobody's perfect, but a true friend should have your back.

If you really care about a friend who has been taking too much from you lately, consider talking to her about it. This will be as difficult as confronting her about a dangerous habit, but again, just remember not to blame her and to make the effort to listen to her rather than simply airing your complaints. Choose your timing wisely as well. Don't, for instance, confront your friend when you've been drinking, when she's about to take a big test or go out on a first date, or when you're about to be surrounded by a bunch of other people (like on your way to lunch or a nighttime event). Even if your friend doesn't react well at first, hopefully in time she will understand your point of view and realize that she needs to change.

She Puts You Down

The Situation

A good friend should lift you up, make you laugh and make you feel happy and confident—not bring you down! Yet sometimes someone close to you might make you feel bad about yourself, whether purposefully or not.

Why It Happens

There are various reasons why your friend might belittle you regularly. She might be putting you down to build herself up, which means she probably suffers from low self-esteem, which can happen to the best of us. On the other hand, if she's being passive-aggressive in her remarks, she might actually be angry at you for something she hasn't explained to you yet, and her frustration is showing in her criticism instead. Of course, it's also possible that she might not even realize she's offending you (or saying anything offensive in the first place).

How to Deal

A so-called friend putting you down is never okay, and you should never stick around while someone is tearing down your self-esteem. If you're close and you just feel that your friend is jealous or insecure, try pointing out her strengths more often so that she takes more pride in herself (and stops focusing on comparing herself to you).

If you think she's angry at you for some reason, let her know that her comments aren't cool and ask if there's something you've done to upset her. Communication is key to any healthy relationship, including a friendship!

If being around a certain friend is hurting your physical or mental health, don't be afraid to walk away. However, if your friend puts you or herself down on a regular basis, this could be a cry for help. Ultimately, it's up to you to distinguish between hopeless situations and ones where your friend simply needs you.

If you find yourself in a situation where your frenemies, actual friends, or actual enemies (such as your misanthropic roommate or the girl whose ex you're now dating) are bringing down your mood or making you feel uncomfortable and unsafe at school, don't be afraid to ask for help. This is especially true if you're being bullied, whether online or in person. In high school, you always had your family home to come back to, even if you were being bullied. In college, however, bullying can be impossible to escape when you're living with the person who is terrorizing you.

Rely on the services your college offers, especially when it comes to campus-related issues such as dorm life, so that you don't have to go through bullying alone. Your RA and on-campus counselors are both amazing resources specializing in conflict resolution! Plus, if the bullying is coming from your roommate, RAs or campus counselors can step in to help you swap rooms. There's no point in sticking around a toxic person, whether you live together or just hang together after classes, so be proactive and stand up for yourself like the strong collegiette you are!

Wellness Check-In: Three Steps to Ditch a Toxic Friend

Whatever highs and lows you encounter in your college friendships, know that they don't have to last forever. Fortunately, the beauty of being on a campus filled with thousands of other undergrads is that you're constantly meeting new people, which means you're constantly faced with opportunities to make new friends! It sounds cheesy, but trust us, there's nothing better than that "aha" moment you experience when you and that girl in your lit class just click. *Voilà!* New friend. It's especially helpful if it's time for you to move on from a not-so-fabulous friend—a toxic one who's bringing you down or even bullying you (it happens!). Not sure how to ditch her?

Explain the Problem

As we've said, communication is always key, especially when things go south in a friendship. Whether she's belittling you, pressuring you, influencing you negatively, or trying to sabotage your life (flirting with your boyfriend, talking behind your back to your mutual friends, etc.), you shouldn't just stand by and let her do so, but you shouldn't walk away right away, either. Sit your friend down and tell her what's bothering you; by bringing it up, you'll give her a chance to address it and hopefully change her ways. You might just salvage your friendship!

Stop Hanging Out One-on-One

If you have "the talk" and she's still causing problems for you, distance yourself by hanging out less and less one-on-one and more and more in groups. That way, you'll have a buffer between the two of you, and you'll both get used to spending less quality time together. Plus, you could find yourself becoming closer to someone else in that group, or she could, which means you'll both be less attached to each other.

Meet New People

College is the ultimate haven for finding new friends, so make an effort to meet new people when you want to branch out. Join a club that interests you, attend on-campus events, join an intramural pick-up game, and chat with classmates before lecture starts. The more people you meet and learn to like, the more chances you'll have to make plans without your toxic friend, and the easier it will be to lead separate lives.

You owe it to yourself to make your college years the absolute best that they can be; the last thing you need is for some catty frenemy or majorly bad influence to get in the way of these awesome four years. Though it takes time, ditching your toxic friend is essential; move on to greener pastures!

Chapter Checklist

- ✓ Don't stay in a relationship for the wrong reasons! If you're with him because you are afraid of being alone, hope you can make him change, or feel too guilty breaking things off, you need to cut the cord for both his sake and yours.
- ✓ If he seems like trouble, don't get involved! Classic signs that he's not boyfriend material include sending late-night booty calls, using pet names constantly, badmouthing exes, and being overprotective of his phone. If he sends player signals, walk away!
- ✓ Know the early signs of abuse so you can spot them in your own relationships as well as your friends': blaming, resentment, and superiority are only a few of the early warning signals to look out for.
- ✓ Frenemies exist in college, too! Ask yourself whether her backhanded compliments or underhandedness were one-time flukes or constant recurrences. If they're the latter, it's time to kick the frenemy to the curb.
- ✓ If your friend is a negative influence, it probably means that you're also a little too tempted by her partying ways or her devil-may-care attitude. Distance yourself from her when

you know the peer pressure could become an issue, such as on weekend nights.

✓ If, on the other hand, your friend is causing trouble just by making jabs at you or belittling you, know that it's likely because she's insecure or jealous. Try casually complimenting her and bringing up her strengths when possible to build up her self-esteem, and let her know if her words really start to hurt.

✓ When you find yourself stuck with a truly toxic friend, take steps to remove yourself from the situation. Communicate openly about the problem so you can give her a chance to fix it, but if it persists, limit your one-on-one time and refocus your efforts onto meeting new people and making friends who will be there for you no matter what!

PART 4

Building a Balanced Social Life

College is *so* much more than just classes, exams, and papers. This is your home for four years, and it's important to take just as much advantage of the social opportunities on campus as the academic ones. The social offerings in college are extensive, and it can be difficult to navigate them all. In the chapters ahead you'll get a taste of the different activities you can participate in as well as learn how to get involved.

Likely you'll find that there is so much you want to do! You'll find yourself signing up for intramural soccer, the school newspaper, and sorority rush all in the same day. It'll be overwhelming, but it'll definitely be worth it. That's why we've also included help on balancing all of your social commitments with your school ones as well as on what to do when you find yourself in over your head.

And with all these fun activities going on, naturally you'll want to share them on your social media accounts (obviously you want to see how many likes your first byline gets you!). But there are a few dos and don'ts of social media now that you're in college, and we'll walk you through those, too!

CHAPTER 14

Extracurriculars

Whether you're a freshman looking to make new friends or an upperclassman looking to boost your resume for an internship or job, clubs are a great way to get relevant experience with other like-minded people. Yes, technically you came to college for the academics, but one of the most rewarding aspects of your college career will likely be your involvement in extracurricular activities.

But with more clubs on campus than TV options on Netflix, it can be difficult to decide which one (or ones) you want to commit your time to. Will joining the mathletes be social suicide? Is varsity way too big of a commitment? Your high school didn't have a student newspaper; is it too late in the game to join a campus publication? Welcome to College Clubs 101; consider this your guide to all things extracurricular!

CAMPUS MEDIA

Whether you consider yourself the voice of your generation, have an unusual knack for grammar, or simply dig writing about your interests, it's never too late to join a campus publication. Read on to discover what type of campus media is best for you!

Student Newspaper

If nothing gets you motivated like an impending deadline, newspaper writing is for you. You'll get the unique opportunity to interview students, professors, and probably even professionals. You'll always be in the know about the biggest news on campus, and your columns might even help shed light on local controversies and issues—or simply make fun of them in the form of political cartoons. You may even grow to love the inverted pyramid style of writing! In the process, you will definitely get close to your editor in some form of love-hate relationship, and you'll probably spend a few late nights cutting your column down to just the right length. Ultimately, your byline will be all over campus, and you'll come out with some amazing clips that you can leverage in internship and job apps. Extra, extra, read all about it!

Campus Magazines

If the school paper isn't for you, there are tons of other publications you can get involved with to showcase your writing. If the pace of your newspaper overwhelms you, more newsy magazines offer you a place to work on longer, more in-depth reads.

Another option is to try reaching out to your school's alumni magazine. Not only do these magazines have a wide circulation, but also through your involvement with one you may meet alumni or faculty who have connections in the field you want to pursue.

If news writing isn't your thing, many colleges also offer literary magazines, which are a great place to showcase your fiction writing or poetry. It's also a terrific resource to have people in the group read your writing and get feedback.

And if your dream job falls more in line with *Glamour* than the *New York Times*, apply to be a campus correspondent or contributing writer with Her Campus (find info on how to apply online at HerCampus.com!), where you can get your work showcased to a national audience and write about everything from "campus cuties" to how to nail a coveted internship.

Campus Radio

Like music? Like the sound of your own voice? Okay, you're perfect for campus radio. Typically, for a campus radio show you'll pick a theme, possibly pick a co-DJ, and curate music and/or interviews to broadcast to your fellow classmates (and also your mom; let's be real). Besides being super fun, having a radio show is also a great way to practice your public speaking skills without having to see whom you're addressing (which eliminates a ton of nerves). Co-DJ-ing a show can also be a great way to make a new friend on campus who has similar musical interests. Whether you have a passion for the music industry or you just really like jamming to Top 40 in your car, working for the campus radio station is a unique college experience that lets you tap into your musical side and share it with your fellow students!

PERFORMANCE GROUPS

So you won your high school talent show four years straight for your incredible singing voice. Or maybe you were the class clown with jokes so good even your AP English teacher couldn't keep from laughing. Or maybe you've just discovered an unexplored passion for dance! All of these are clear signs that you should join a performance group on campus. Which one, you ask? Read on to discover how you can become a class act!

A Cappella Ensembles

You've seen *Glee*, you've seen *The Voice*, and you want in on that amazing life-is-like-a-musical experience. The daunting part: in a cappella, there are no musical instruments to augment your voice. You may have to make funny clicking sounds with your mouth that would sound awkward in public if they were not performed in the unique context of a cappella. You may get to sing a solo with a group of your peers supporting you musically and a sea of cheering students before you on the quad. You will undoubtedly get close to your fellow a cappella mates as you practice songs throughout the year, and you will definitely get over any stage fright you might have. Your life might not always be like a musical, but with a cappella, it can be pretty pitch perfect.

Dance Groups

Most colleges have a variety of dance groups on campus, so whether you've been doing pliés since age three or you prefer to bust your moves to Britney Spears in the comfort of your bedroom, there's probably a group that matches your skill set and level. Joining a dance team is a great way to both socialize and exercise! Plus, who doesn't love dance costumes? Just don't drive your roommate up the wall by practicing in your dorm room to the same song thirty times a day.

Four Bad Reasons to Join a Club

Extracurriculars can enrich your college experience unlike many other things, but it's important that you're in them for the right reasons—that is, not these:

- You think the club will look good on your resume.
- The guy you have a crush on is in the club.
- All your friends are joining it.
- Your friend runs it and is guilting you into joining.

How to Start a Club

Is your college missing a club that you would love to be a part of? Start it yourself!

Recruit Potential Members

Before you do anything official, ask your peers if this would be something they'd be interested in joining. It helps to have a foundation of club members to launch your club so it won't be you alone trying to recruit members.

Register Your Organization

There should be a form on your college's website that gets the ball rolling on the registration process for your organization. While this may be a bit tedious, don't skip this step! Registering your club will provide you with great resources, including promotion, validity, a legitimate location to meet, a website domain, and in some cases, a budget from the student activities office.

Promote Your Club

Post about your club on social media, send e-mail over mailing list servers, chalk sidewalks and walkways, and hang up flyers around your dorm so that people know about your new organization.

CULTURAL AND RELIGIOUS GROUPS

In college it can be hard to preserve the cultural and religious aspects of your home life. Joining a club of people who have a similar background is a great way not only to celebrate your heritage, but also to expose other people to it (or discover a new culture!).

Foreign Language Club

Whether you want to practice your foreign-language speaking skills or are just really into learning about other cultures (and eating international food!), a foreign language club is a great opportunity for both. Most colleges probably have clubs for the most popular foreign languages in the United States—Spanish, French, German, etc.—but now might be the time to break out of your shell and learn about a completely new language and culture! Perhaps your school has a Russian club, or a Vietnamese club. Whichever one you join, your language skills (and your palate) are sure to benefit!

Religious Groups

Used to practicing your religion every week with Mom and Dad? Seeking out a religious group can bring you back in touch with your faith. Religious groups will give you people to celebrate religious holidays with when going home to your family isn't an option. They will also provide you with a network of people who not only practice the same religion as you do but also prioritize religion as much as you do, and who want to worship with others. Many groups also create communities to provide spiritual wisdom for each other or even just to have social events.

Cultural Dance Groups

Joining a dance group tied to your culture (or another culture you're interested in) is an incredible way to learn and to educate audiences during your performances. The groups typically aim to educate the university and community about their culture through a combination of music, art, and dance. Some groups try to modernize traditional dance and music, where others aim to preserve the tradition and share it with a larger group. Even if you have two left feet, checking out a cultural dance group performance on campus is a must before graduation.

PROFESSIONAL SOCIETIES

If you want access to major professional networks and a fast track to your dream career, you should definitely check out the professional societies on campus! Some of the following clubs are branches of national societies; if your school does not currently have a branch, you can start one yourself and earn major leadership points in the process. There are professional Greek organizations for people interested in all sorts of fields, such as psychology, music, and chemical engineering. If you're looking to join an organization that will allow you to bond with fellow students with whom you share a common interest, but you want something more than just a club, a professional fraternity or sorority might be a good fit for you. Read on to learn more about these groups!

National Honor Fraternities

If you join a professional Greek organization that relates to your future career path, your current brothers or sisters as well as alumni can help you out professionally both before and after graduation through networking, resume critiques, and industry insider knowledge. Many involve recruitment, pledging, and dues similar to Greek social organizations, but tend to be smaller in size since the interests of those who join are so specific, which can help you bond with your brothers and sisters even more.

Public Relations Society of America (PRSA)

If you're interested in PR, your campus's branch of PRSA is where you want to be. This group offers internship listings, national competitions within the society, networking opportunities, and tons of resources for learning more about the field of public relations. If your school doesn't have a chapter, you can start one!

Ed2010

If you're interested in the magazine industry, this national club is for you. Ed2010 chapters host panels with professional writers, serve as outlets to visiting national writers and editors, and facilitate resume critiques. If your campus does not have an Ed2010 chapter, you can start one and gain major leadership experience in the process.

Three Perks of Being a Campus Tour Guide

Serving as a tour guide at your school comes with a host of benefits that not all extracurriculars can offer, such as:

- Public speaking experience
- The chance to learn new things about your college (maybe you'll find a new fave study spot!)
- A chance to make money (most colleges pay their tour guides)

Which Clubs Are Good for My Resume?

You want extracurriculars to impress your future employers, but what if you don't know who those employers are or what kind of job you're going to want? We know that deciding on a post-college career path can be stressful, but that doesn't mean that choosing your extracurriculars has to be. Here are the most useful activities for any career path.

Public service: There is never going to be an employer who is turned off by your philanthropic efforts. You really can't go wrong by doing right.

Greek life: Despite their party reputation, listing your Greek affiliation may give you an immediate connection to your interviewer (what if she was also a Tri Delt?). Bonus points if you have a leadership position within your sorority and can refer to the great communication and organization skills you learned through it.

Debate teams: They're not just for the politically minded; public speaking is a skill anyone can use. You'll learn to convey your thoughts clearly and understand different points of view.

Clubs that relate to your major: If you have an idea of what field you want to go into, you should definitely seek out a related organization. Pre-professional groups are also great if you don't have a major yet; maybe you'll love the marketing club so much that you decide to change majors! If your major doesn't have a student organization, you can always start one yourself.

Resident life: Being an RA will teach you how to handle a plethora of issues, from roommate fights to illegal substance use. It will give you hands-on experience with counseling, organization, conflict management, and leadership—all things that will come in handy for your career.

Peer tutoring: You'll show your employers that you can effectively explain challenging concepts to others.

School newspaper: Not only will you sharpen your writing skills, but you'll also learn editing, critical thinking, and how to operate under tight deadlines, which is standard in the workplace.

Tour guide: Employers will love that you stepped up to a leadership role on campus. These positions are very competitive, and the fact that your school wanted you to represent them might make companies think that you could be a good representative for them as well.

Resume Booster

As you can see, there are many things that will boost your resume, no matter what field you go into. If you're passionate about something, no matter what it is, your passion will show during an interview and reflect well on you, so you shouldn't hesitate to put the groups you're excited about on your resume!

SPORTS

If you're a high school athlete, you're faced with the decision to play or not to play sports in college. For some, this choice is clear-cut. For others, however, it can be more complicated. There are divisions within college athletics and even more options beyond just the varsity level. Fortunately, if you're up to play, there will be some level for you!

Varsity

Varsity sports can be Division I, II, or III within the NCAA depending on your school. The schools themselves choose divisions based on student enrollment, financial estimates, and support from fans. Division I is the most competitive—students must be recruited before matriculation freshman year—and also offers the most generous financial scholarships for sports participation. Division II is a little more academics-focused, with a rigid restriction on the amount of financial aid that can be awarded to athletes and the opportunity for "walking on" the team, bypassing formal recruitment prior to matriculation. Division III sports are the least competitive on the varsity level, and this division does not offer financial aid scholarships for athletic ability. That being said, Division III sports still tend to be much more competitive than intramural or club sports, and will still require a significant time commitment and athletic ability.

Club

The major draw for club sports is that they function almost entirely outside of the university's athletic department and are largely student-run. Club sports offer a balance between competition and fun where you can commit to a team without sacrificing academics. Club sports at your school will most likely compete against sports teams at other schools similar to the varsity level, but tend to maintain a less competitive atmosphere and lower commitment level.

Intramural

Intramural sports offer a lot of options to athletes. Most schools have intramural programs that are divided into levels from beginner to advanced. That way, anyone who signs up can participate. Most teams start with groups of friends who live in the same dorm or have classes together. Why not get together a beginner team and try playing a sport you haven't before? Intramural sports are a great way to continue playing a sport you would rather not give up, meet new people, or bond with friends in another club or sorority. Many schools have Greek-only leagues reserved for just fraternity and sorority teams to compete as well. Leagues are also divided into all-male, all-female, or coed groups.

CAMPUS LIFE

You'll be living here for the next few years; you might as well have an impact on your university! Whether you want to get involved with student government, promote your school to pre-freshmen, or just have an impact on your dorm, campus life is a great way to share your love of your school and have a hand in making these four years what you want them to be. Plus it's also a way to hone your leadership skills, which will be valuable for the rest of your life.

Student Government

Student government is a great way to lead your student body and make changes at your school. Your involvement can vary depending on which aspects of campus life interest you the most. For example, many schools feature opportunities to run for dorm council, class council, or as a representative of student life.

Residence Life

Make a difference in your day-to-day life by getting involved with Residence Life. Whether you get involved on the dorm level or throughout all of the campus, you will do things like organize fun events, coordinate group service projects, address community issues, and work to promote happiness among your fellow collegiettes (and colle-gents!).

Campus Ambassadors/Tour Guides

Love your college? Are you surprisingly good at walking backwards? Being a tour guide is for you! This competitive position on campus is a great way to share your school pride with potential students and make an impact on their college admissions process. A good tour guide or campus ambassador can make or break a high school student's experience on your campus, so this is a position that's great for bubbly, outgoing, upbeat collegiettes!

JUST FOR FUN

Always wanted to go skydiving on the weekends? Have a hankering to wear a clown nose around campus? Are you an avid but closeted squirrel fan? While getting involved in normal school clubs such as student government and the university newspaper may be your initial thought when you land on campus in the fall, why not branch out and join the weirdest club you can find? Every college student is unique, and these student organizations at universities across the country sure fit with that adjective.

Foodie Clubs

The social clubs that celebrate eating on campus can range from groups that celebrate their love of pizza crust, to groups that sample different cheeses at every meeting, host cooking lessons, or celebrate a specific cultural food type. Not only will you potentially expand your palate, but you'll also seriously bond with people in your club, because what better way to make friends than by breaking bread with them?

Game Clubs

Whether you prefer live action role-playing games like Assassin or more obscure games like tiddlywinks, there is a club for you. Clubs like these will host larger games throughout the semester or allow you to play every time you meet.

Animal-Related Clubs

These kinds of groups aren't philanthropically working to protect endangered species or help local puppies get adopted.

No, fun animal groups are for more obscure things, like squirrel-watching. Seriously, you may be able to find a club that centers around feeding squirrels every week. Maybe something more traditional like bird-watching or nature walking is up your alley? You can find that too!

Optimistic Clubs

Love hugs? You may find a club that does little more than offer free hugs around campus. Are you always happy (or do you aim to be that way)? Some campuses have clubs that promote happiness in the simplest of ways, like chalking uplifting words around campus.

Special Interest

On campus, you have a much better chance of finding people who share your more obscure interests, like an obsession with moustaches or an appreciation for clown noses. It's hard to believe, but there are colleges with clubs just for those activities. But you can also find groups for more widely appreciated hobbies, like Quidditch or skydiving.

Wellness Check-In: Four Ways Participating in Extracurriculars Can Help Your Mental Health

1. Clubs will be a fun distraction from the stresses of college classes and help you unwind in a positive way.
2. A study at the University of Exeter Medical School found that volunteering is associated with lower incidences of depression. So helping people really does help you out!

3. Being part of a club or organization that connects you back with your culture or religion can help combat homesickness and give you a community on campus.

4. Clubs can be empowering. Clubs in college are run by students rather than faculty. Not only does this make you feel really independent and responsible, but it usually allows the group to have more productive and open conversations as well. Student-run organizations can be a great opportunity for you to take on responsibility.

Chapter Checklist

✓ Find the clubs for you. Decide what area or areas are of interest (media, performance, etc.) and check out a wide variety of clubs by reading about them online, checking out their meetings, and attending their events.

✓ If you can't find your club, start it. The paperwork for this should be on your Student Life website.

✓ Reap the mental health benefits of getting involved on campus!

✓ Have fun!

CHAPTER 15

Greek Life

Depending on where you go to school, you may have heard that joining a sorority is an all-access pass to a huge group of friends, awesome parties, an active social life, and even a huge network you can tap into professionally after college. On the flip side, you may have heard that sorority girls are catty, competitive partiers who will make you stay up all night, and eat live goldfish to become a member. What does joining a sorority really entail? From the rush process and college life as a Greek student to becoming an alumna, Her Campus can walk you through all things Greek so you can decide if joining a sorority is for you!

SHOULD YOU RUSH?

Sorority recruitment: For some, this means waking up early to converse with strangers for hours while you judge one another on appearance and personality. To others, it means the opportunity to meet tons of super cool, like-minded girls on campus and begin to build brand-new lifelong friendships under the umbrella of a strong national organization. Whether you're on the fence about joining a Greek organization on campus or you've already started a Pinterest board for all of the new sorority gear you want (pending which house you join, of course!), recruitment is the best way to decide if Greek life is right for you and, if you join, which house feels most like home to you.

Just because you rush doesn't mean you have to pledge (commit yourself to join a particular sorority). If you don't feel that any house is a great fit, you can drop out at any time or choose not to pledge. And if you do feel that you fit in at a particular chapter, then you are in for what many consider to be an amazing experience with a whole new group of friends.

NAVIGATING SORORITY RUSH

So you signed up for rush and you're ready to test out the waters of Greek life. Congratulations! The decision to participate in the rush process is a major one for any collegiette, as it requires time and stamina (you'll be talking to a LOT of girls!) and may lead you to join an organization that will have a major impact on your college career and quite possibly the rest of your life. But it can be difficult to navigate, so we'll take you through all the rounds.

Pre-Recruitment

Enthusiastic Greek friends and relatives may have already bombarded you with advice about rush, giving you pointers on what to say, how to dress, and how to get those letters of recommendation.

You might be thinking, "Letters of recommendation? I thought I was applying for a sisterhood, not a job!" Don't stress! This is simply a form filled out by an alumna of a particular sorority recommending you for that sorority. These forms, which can be found on each sorority's national website, require information about your grades, test scores, volunteer work, extracurricular activities, and hobbies. They're usually submitted along with two photographs (one headshot and one of your full body).

By no means does everyone need to worry about these letters. In general, if you are headed for any school with a reputation for having a competitive recruitment process, you can assume that getting letters of recommendation for every house is basically essential. At schools without a competitive rush reputation, however, it can be hard to tell whether you should get them for every house, just a few houses, or none at all. If you know any older girl well enough, feel free to ask her. At some schools Greek life is not treated as such a big deal, and a letter may seem like overkill.

Round One: Open House

A Rho Gamma, or older sorority girl who has temporarily disaffiliated from her chapter to be your guide, will lead you and a bunch of other PNMs (potential new members) from house to house (never admitting which is hers!). At each house, you'll be greeted by high-energy, screaming, dancing sorority girls. One will grab your arm (seemingly out of nowhere) and you'll chat for a few minutes until another sister approaches you. After about twenty minutes, the rush chair will make a speech, and you might hear a funny story or do a short activity before you're ushered out. At the end of the day, you'll write down which chapters you liked the best and cut a few houses, and the sorority girls will do the same with the PNMs.

Round Two: House Tours

Round Two activities vary by school—sometimes they will include a craft, a philanthropy presentation, or a skit—but typically this round will involve a tour of each sorority house. You will still talk to more than one girl—usually about three—before taking a tour of the house and learning more about the chapter's activities and structure. For example, you may hear a presentation on the chapter's national and local philanthropies, or learn about how much it would cost to live there. Again, you rank the sororities you saw at the end of the day and cut a few more houses.

Round Three: Skit

Again, Round Three activities vary, and many schools do not do a skit. If your school doesn't do one, this could be called the "Philanthropy Round," and in some cases house tours occur during Round Three. If there is a skit, you will talk to two or three girls before watching the most recent pledge class of each chapter put on a hilarious performance, often involving pop culture references and songs. This is a great chance to get to know the personality of each house, so you can gauge better where you'll feel most comfortable. You'll rank the sororities again at the end of the day, and again will cut some.

Round Four: Preference

This round is the most serious; you only talk to one girl for the entire time—a full hour at most schools—and the dress code is usually cocktail attire. It's all about the traditions, principles, and values of each chapter in this round. You'll hear from the girls about what their sorority means to them, and see a ceremony that emphasizes the essence of each house. Often there is a presentation involving the seniors, and you learn a lot about the traditions of each chapter. At the end of the day you "pref" the sororities in order of where you'd most like to pledge, and you are matched up through a computer system to a house.

What Happens If You Don't Get Into a Sorority

After weeks of preparation, strutting around campus in your favorite dresses and meeting with girl after girl, it's finally the end of sorority rush. Throughout the process, you had your eye set on one house, and you hoped that the odds were in your favor. But what happens when your top pick passes you by, or you're left bid-less altogether? Although it may be difficult to deal with at first, you *will* get through it (we promise)!

First, don't let it ruin your year. It's normal to feel disappointed and upset, but letting not getting into a sorority define the rest of your year is a different story. Second, you should definitely join other clubs. There are *plenty* of opportunities to meet friends on campus; Greek life is just one of the many outlets to consider. To find the perfect club for you, start by attending organization fairs or looking online to see which clubs are offered at your school.

Most importantly, don't let the jealousy get to you. You and your BFF decided to rush together, and now you're left without a sorority while she received a bid from your top pick (yikes). When it comes to rushing, it's easy to take things personally (*why'd they choose her and not me?*), but for the sake of your sanity and happiness, you can't let jealousy get the best of you.

WHAT SORORITY LIFE IS LIKE

Got a bid and wondering if you should accept? Consider these pros and cons.

PRO: You'll expand your social circles and meet tons of new people.

CON: Between Greek-sponsored events, pledging, Greek Week, parties, and informal get-togethers, sororities can be time-consuming.

PRO: You have a network of girls to help you with your classes and to build career connections with.

CON: Given the cost to live in the house, dues, Greek swag, gifts for your sorority little sister once you have one, and all those t-shirts, sororities can be expensive.

PRO: You'll find a group of girls you can not only be comfortable with but also do things with, such as participate in philanthropy and do intramurals.

CON: Some sororities promote hazing, which is when a group pressures you to do something that is potentially dangerous or can damage your mental, physical, or emotional health. While hazing is getting a serious crackdown on the sorority level and the university level, unfortunately it still exists at some schools.

Pledging

Pledging a sorority involves many different activities and meetings, many of which are mandatory. This means that for most collegiettes, pledging ends up being a significant time commitment.

New members spend a lot of time learning about the different aspects of their sorority. By the end of the pledging period, they're expected to know about not only their sorority's mission and values, but also all of its current members. Many sororities even have a sort of final entrance exam on what new pledges have learned. Some sororities will expect pledges to learn miscellaneous facts about the sorority and its members and will quiz them on such details.

Along with the time pledges spend learning about their sororities, they are typically also expected to attend events such as mandated study times, weekly meetings, and other social activities to get to know their sisters and the organization they just joined. But it's fun! The older girls dote on you, and one time in particular during pledging is the best week ever (for pledges)—Big/Little Week!

Hazing

Hazing forces pledges to participate in activities that are specifically designed to make them uncomfortable in some way, and it can lead to dangerous outcomes. Hazing could be anything from being forced to drink to having your naked body judged by your future sisters or even fraternity brothers.

Hazing typically occurs because the sisters think it's a bonding experience; it's thought to be a pain that brings pledges together through shared coping. For the sororities, it also brings about conformity and obedience—and people participate out of fear of rejection from the sorority. The cycles of hazing continue because sisters who survive hazing often believe that if they survived it, their new pledges need to as well—and occasionally consider it revenge for their own hazing. However, none of these excuses are valid reasons for hazing.

Hazing does still happen in some sororities, but more and more schools are cracking down on it. Many colleges have zero-tolerance policies on hazing and also use other methods to prevent it. If a university suspects hazing, the organization at hand will be investigated and can face suspension.

If you find yourself feeling pressured by your new sisters, call the Anti-Hazing Hotline (1-888-NOT-HAZE). Many national sororities (as well as universities) have hazing hotlines where you can call and report an incident. To learn more about what constitutes hazing, check out your chapter's (and your school's) anti-hazing policy.

Greek Family: Bigs and Littles

One super important part of the pledging process for the majority of sororities is the big-little relationship. At some point during pledging, each pledge will get a "big," or "big sister," to guide her through the pledging process. Most sororities even have a Big/Little Week during which the big showers her little with gifts before revealing who she is on the last day. Gifts typically include sorority memorabilia and tons of candy. Perks of the week can include rides to and from class from fraternity pledges, meal deliveries, and having your room decorated by your new big.

Pledges' bigs act as their go-to person whenever they have questions or concerns during pledging. They are supposed to make their littles feel special and welcome, and most do a pretty great job of it.

Getting to Know Your Pledge Class

You and the other girls in your pledge class will be doing a lot together while learning the ropes of your sorority. At least once a week, your pledge class will meet to learn the traditions, secrets, and rules of the sorority in a class setting. Your pledge class will be your support system—you'll all be going through the same experience together and bond with newfound sisterhood.

GREEK SOCIAL LIFE

Most of what you've heard about Greek life is probably about parties, but there's more to it than ragers! There is a wide variety of different social events available for members of Greek life.

Mixers

Mixers are between a sorority and a fraternity and are a great way to bond with a fraternity in a smaller setting than a big, open party. Often a sorority and a fraternity will have a long-standing relationship, and the girls and guys will be friends all throughout college.

Formals

Missing your high school prom, when you got to dress up in a poofy pink dress and dance the night away with your BFFs? Worry no more; if you're in a sorority or have a close friend or boyfriend in a frat, your first college formal is right around the corner. Think of a formal as the college version of a high school dance (minus the cheesy decorations and teacher supervision). You can forget about homecoming court drama and choosing a dress that follows your school's strict dress code.

Crush Parties

Crush parties are the closest things sororities have to open parties. Crush parties happen once or twice a year and are an opportunity for sorority girls to invite their crushes (literally) or friends not in the house to a sorority-hosted event. Depending on your sorority, you will have a small number of invites (think one to four) for each event, and many sororities let you purchase additional ones.

Fraternity Parties

Fraternity parties can be enjoyed by those in and out of Greek life, before and after you join a sorority. Fraternity parties are typically parties held in a big ground floor or basement of the house, jam-packed with college students reeking of beer and sweat.

LIVING IN THE SORORITY HOUSE

Moving into a sorority house is like entering an alternate-universe girl world, and it's a culture shock for even the most frilly, flirty Sorority Sallys among us. Get ready for living in a sorority house by following these lessons that sorority girls before you had to learn the hard way.

Buy Yourself a Pair of Earplugs

Seriously, sorority houses are LOUD. Who knew girls could produce as much noise as they do? From the second the earliest riser gets up (at roughly 6 A.M.) to the instant the hardest-working engineer or craziest partygoer falls into bed (again, roughly 6 A.M.), a sorority house is comparable in noise level to the front row of a concert. If you find that all that noise isn't the best studying (or sleeping) soundtrack, try getting yourself a pair of earplugs—they work wonders!

You No Longer Have a Car (If Anyone Asks)

Bringing your car to school is super convenient, right? But when you move into a sorority house, a girl with a car becomes a resource more valuable than the rarest African diamond—and just as exploited. If you bring your car to a sorority house, you'll constantly be hit up for rides all over campus. Trust us, leave the wheels at home—the extra walk to class will do you good, anyway.

Catch the Early-Bird Special or Go Hungry

More often than not, as soon as the sorority chef puts out the food, girls stampede into the kitchen to get their fill of chicken masala before everyone else. And shortly thereafter, every last morsel is cleared and the sisters are left to snack on cereal or leftover fruit salad. Lesson: if you want good, hot food, eat when the food goes out, not necessarily when you want to eat.

HOW GREEK LIFE CAN HELP YOUR CAREER

If you've already decided going Greek on campus is right for you, get excited, because the perks of Greek life don't end on graduation day. Greek life can actually make a strong impact on your career long after college is over!

On the lowest level of career help is simply putting your sorority name on your resume (especially if you can amp it up with a leadership role). You may find that amongst hundreds of resumes, yours stuck out simply because the interviewer was in the same sorority. Okay, but you could say this about any club; two people could bond over being in the French club! However, being in a sorority tends to elicit stronger feelings, because in many cases it was a large part of the person's college experience.

Much more significant are the tangible resources your sorority can offer, such as:

- A dedicated LinkedIn group that can connect you with alumnae from or outside of your school who are established in their careers.
- Formal career networking opportunities, both virtual (online) and in person.
- Alumnae events where you can mix and mingle with alums (and here's a tip: actually talk to them! Make connections and swap info!).

Wellness Check-In: Seven Ways Joining a Sorority Can Help You Get the Most Out of College

Joining a sorority can really make your college experience. Here are seven ways a sorority helps you make the most of your four years.

- **You make more friends!** You don't have to give up the friends you made initially, but you'll definitely end up making a whole bunch of new ones.
- **You will connect with older students.** Meeting older girls can be hard, but having girls in the pledge classes above you will be a great resource for advice on navigating your specific college, what classes to take, and other very specific ways to have a great experience on campus.
- **You'll meet more guys.** Mixers, philanthropic partnerships with fraternities, and Greek Week will introduce you to more guys than you'd probably ever meet on your own on campus. You might even meet a potential boyfriend!
- **You'll get even more involved on campus.** You might even get a leadership role to add to your resume!
- **Particularly at big schools, you'll get to enjoy the benefits of a small community of like-minded women you can bond with and learn from.**
- **You'll have an active social calendar.** You'll never be bored when you're in a sorority—if you stay involved, there will always be either something to plan (like a crush party) or something to do (like a philanthropic event).
- **You'll have a larger network of resources for internships and post-graduation jobs.**

Chapter Checklist

✓ Research Greek life at your school long before rush starts to get a feel for how important it is to student life.

✓ Review the rush process to know what to expect when you open the doors to the sorority house and think through what to talk about and what to wear.

✓ Take advantage of every opportunity once you're in a sorority. Enjoy the social events—the mixers, crush parties, and formals. You won't have many opportunities after graduation to participate in a blacklight party! But also participate in philanthropic events and networking events. Greek life is what you make of it.

✓ Reap all the career benefits offered to you in Greek life. These are invaluable connections!

CHAPTER 16

Juggling Social Life and Academics

College isn't only about classes and exams. You learn just as much about yourself and growing up outside of the classroom as you do inside the classroom. To get the most from your college experience, you need to enjoy your time out of the lecture hall. But you also have to strike a balance between a burgeoning social life and a fulfilling academic life. Your social life is getting busier because your friends are right there, and your workload is getting harder and more time-consuming at the college level. To succeed in college, you have to learn to manage your time, avoid procrastination, and know when you've taken on too much.

TIME MANAGEMENT AND EFFECTIVE STUDYING

Chances are that finding time to be social won't be your problem at school—that typically comes pretty easily (and, truth be told, you shouldn't sacrifice it)—and your lessons in time management will be associated with schoolwork. To manage your time and not find yourself swamped in work during midterms and finals, follow these tips.

Plan Ahead

Most professors will provide you with a syllabus the first day of class that outlines every assignment you have for the semester. Get organized and add all of the important dates to your planner. On top of that, put warnings in your agenda for the week before a major test or paper so you're thinking ahead.

Find a Study Buddy

Find a study partner or group that meets on a weekly or biweekly basis to talk through the material. These people will also keep you accountable and prevent you from slipping behind in your work.

Actually Follow Your Schedule and Assignments

It's understandable that you may fall behind, but do what you can to catch up before it's too late. Skipping a few readings here and there adds up and will have you feeling like you're drowning at the end of the semester when you have 400 pages to read.

Don't Cram

Shoving weeks' worth of information into your brain in such a short span of time is not conducive to actually remembering the material in the future for a final or for a higher-level class. Plus, cramming has a terrible effect on your stress levels.

Don't Multitask

By dividing your attention among so many different tasks, either the quality of your work or your efficiency is bound to suffer. Catching up on your favorite show while you do your French homework may seem like a great way of managing your time, but it's really not. So instead of taking two hours to write one sentence of your paper because you keep stopping to look at pictures of cute puppies on Pinterest (not that we blame you), turn off the distractions around you and focus solely on your work. Make a deal with yourself that you'll finish all your work before watching the latest episode in your Netflix binge so that you'll be more motivated to get your work done and will have something to look forward to while doing it.

Study Tools

Programs like Audacity, which you can use to record all kinds of audio files, allow you to speed up audio and video so you can watch it twice as fast. If you're slogging your way through a boring chapter in your econ textbook, see if there are lectures or videos available on YouTube that might explain the material in a more exciting and understandable manner. Try the Pomodoro Technique: This technique states that whenever you're working on something that takes up a large chunk of time, it's most efficient to spend twenty-five minutes working on the task, then take a five-minute break. After four twenty-five-minute chunks, take a fifteen- to thirty-minute break instead.

Choose the Right Environment

Make sure you choose a spot that meets your study needs. If you realize that you just end up falling asleep whenever you try to read in bed, don't try to convince yourself that this night will be different; instead, hit up a study lounge and get your work done there. If utter silence stifles your creativity, try writing that essay in a coffee shop instead of the library.

Practice Active Studying

By utilizing numerous active study strategies, such as talking over the concepts with classmates, drawing out graphs, and doing practice problems, you'll understand the material better than if you just reread the textbook.

Sleep

You're not effectively managing your time if you're sacrificing sleep. Your brain will not perform at its best when you're sleep-deprived, so that is totally counterproductive when studying.

Utilize Available Resources

There are countless resources on every college campus that can help you study, from practice exams and review sessions to tutors. And don't forget—professors are resources that you should definitely utilize, too. Talking to your professor during office hours before an exam to review or after an exam to go over your mistakes will not only help you understand the material better, but it'll also show the professor that you care about his or her class.

How to Avoid Checking Social Media When You're Studying

If your social media addiction is too strong to fight on your own, there are tricks you can employ to help you stay focused. When typing up a paper or study guide in Word, use Focus view (View >> Focus/Full Screen) on a Mac or Read Mode (View >> Read Mode) on a PC. This will put your document in full screen and hide all toolbars that don't pertain to editing. Also, turn off Wi-Fi. If you are doing something that doesn't necessitate Internet connection (e.g., typing up your notes, working on a paper), shut off the connection. Other applications, such as SelfControl for Macs or Cold Turkey for PCs, let you block yourself out of certain websites for a specified period of time. These apps are strict—even if you restart your computer or delete the app, the websites will still remain blocked for your set period of time.

WHAT TO DO WHEN YOU'VE TAKEN ON TOO MUCH

If you find yourself in hot water, here are some tips to lighten your load and get you back on track.

Dropping a Class

When you've never had the opportunity to drop a class before, it may seem daunting or lazy to do so. But sometimes dropping a class can be the smartest move you make all semester.

Typically in your credit-heavy schedule, there's that one class you just can't stand: the monotone professor, the painfully dull readings, the grueling exams, not to mention your terrible grade on the first assignment. With these unbearable courses, sometimes dropping a class is your only option. But where should you draw the line between a class you need to drop and a class worth charging through with a (forced) smile?

When the Course Load Is Too Much

It's important to trust your instincts and know when enough is enough. The syllabus should generally provide a clear idea of what to expect and what level the academic rigor will be. It's okay, and important, to acknowledge when you're in over your head. If this class is mandatory and wasn't too hard to get into, try scheduling it with less demanding classes next semester instead. If it's not mandatory and the amount of work needed for this class will drag down your grades in other classes, forget it. It won't be worth having the grades in your mandatory classes slipping.

When You Fail the First Test

It's normal not to ace your first exam of the semester—you're not used to your professor's exam structure, and the subject matter can be hard to get used to. But what about when you bomb a test so badly that you can't recover? Alas, it may be time to pull the plug on this course. But before you do, make sure you try out all of your options. Before you drop the class (particularly a mandatory one), talk to your professor or a TA about how you could potentially improve your grade.

If it seems as if all hope is lost, it may be time to say adios to that class. If this horrid class is a requirement, try taking the course over the summer, when you can focus solely on this material.

When You Can't Stand Your Professor

Whether it's his constant pacing around the classroom or her lame jokes, there's something about your professor that makes you want to say goodbye and good riddance to this class. Before you do anything drastic (a.k.a. dropping the course), let's tap into your psyche to figure out why you don't like this professor. Although you may despise his or her quirks or you heard that your roommate's boyfriend's best friend didn't like the professor last semester, it's time to take a deep breath and stay the course (pun intended).

However, some situations make dropping a class necessary. If you can't understand your professor or if he or she goes on random rants instead of teaching you the material, you may want to think about dropping. If this class is mandatory, make sure you can take the same course with a different professor.

Extensions

While extensions can have kind of a slacker association, sometimes it's not a bad thing to ask for one. One good reason for an extension is if you want to add components that will dramatically improve your assignment.

It's also worth asking for an extension on an assignment if you are struggling with unclear directions or if you do not have sufficient resources to complete the assignment, such as if the assignment assumes a level of background knowledge that not everyone in the class has. This could be affecting the entire class, so expressing your concerns to your professor may be the best way to go.

Being studious and hardworking may prove to be an advantage if you need an extension: Professors would much rather give an extension to someone with a consistent track record for turning in good work on time than someone who is known for sloppy work that tends to come in late.

One of the main things to keep in mind when you're planning on asking for an extension is that you shouldn't wait until the very last minute to do so. It will look as if you've procrastinated, which won't leave a good impression on your professor. If you ask early and provide a good reason, you are halfway to your extension.

Asking for an extension may seem scary, but it's a whole lot better than failing the assignment or the class altogether! The worst that your professor can say is that you can't have an extension, but it's worth a try.

How to Actually Ask for an Extension

Asking for an extension can be scary, but not with this straight-to-the point e-mail. Avoid making up excuses (especially ones that make note of your social life or disorganization) or asking at the last second, and you'll have the best chance of getting an extension.

Dear Professor _____,

I've been having a hard time finding sources for my term paper, and in order for it to be the best it can be, I could really use a little extra time to research and write it. Would it be possible to have an extension for a few days?

Please let me know if you would like for me to meet with you during your office hours to discuss this further.

Sincerely,

[Your name]

Moving Exams

Since professors give out syllabi at the beginning of the semester, you should already have the exam dates for most, if not all, of your final tests. Start looking at your finals schedule: Do you have three papers due in a twenty-four-hour period? Do you have two finals scheduled at the same time? Start talking to your professors at least a couple of weeks in advance if you notice some conflicts in your schedule. Professors typically provide instructions for accommodating students in their syllabi, so be sure to consult that document first. Additionally, check with an administrator or professor to see if your college has any formal processes you need to go through to get a final paper extension or an exam time change.

Taking a Course Pass/Fail

If you have too much on your plate, consider making one of your classes "pass/fail" if that option is available. Translation? Instead of receiving a letter grade, you will either pass the course or fail it—and it won't affect your GPA.

Auditing a Class

Auditing a class means that you don't have to write papers or take exams. If you're interested in auditing a class, talk to your academic advisor for more details, such as whether the class will show up on your transcript. Since you won't receive any college credit, make sure you're actually passionate about the subject, because you're still required to attend each class. And be sure to find out your school's policy on withdrawing or absence from class. You'll want to know how it will appear on your record if you withdraw or stop attending a class you're auditing midway through the semester.

Wellness Check-In: Seven Ways All-Nighters Are Bad for Your Health and Grades

All-nighters aren't good for your health or your academic success.

1. Students who pull frequent all-nighters are found to have lower GPAs.
2. Pulling all-nighters decreases your productivity.
3. Skimping on sleep decreases your mental sharpness.
4. Sleep deprivation from all-nighters can decrease long-term learning and memorization.
5. All-nighters are often fueled by Adderall and caffeine, both of which can have detrimental health effects when used improperly or excessively.
6. Sleep deprivation can lead to overeating, and therefore weight gain.
7. Exhaustion can cause a weakened immune system, depression, and irritability.

Chapter Checklist

- ✓ Manage your time effectively to avoid all-nighters and getting behind on your work.
- ✓ Try out different study methods to discover your most effective way of studying.
- ✓ Plan your semester out so you know what your workload will be each week.
- ✓ Do not be afraid to make changes if you're overwhelmed.
- ✓ Stay healthy while studying by eating right and getting a good night's sleep.

CHAPTER 17

Social Media Dos and Don'ts

Social media can be a ton of fun. These platforms are also a great way to stay in touch with your home friends, so naturally you want them to see how much fun you're having in college! And when you put up a photo of your friend doing a keg stand, the only thing that crosses your mind is how many likes it'll get, not what a potential employer will think of it in four years.

In today's world, you always need to think about your social media presence, as annoying as that is. Something you post online today could come back to haunt you down the line, particularly when it comes to scoring coveted internships and jobs.

KEEPING A PROFESSIONAL AND CLEAN SOCIAL MEDIA PRESENCE

So that you don't self-sabotage your shot at those jobs and internships, heed these tips to keep your social media presence squeaky clean.

Keep Your Privacy Settings High

Especially while applying for jobs and internships, keep your profiles on lock. You should definitely not have public profiles that include inappropriate details. It's not just photos—everything on your page should be rated "G." Don't use curse words in your favorite quote section, and don't post moody or whiny status updates (you shouldn't be venting through the Internet, anyway!). Facebook gives you an option to block your name from coming up entirely, so take advantage of that if you wish (Account >> Privacy Settings >> Search). If you're constantly tweeting, Twitter also gives you an option to make your tweets visible to only your followers (Settings >> Tweet Privacy >> Protect My Tweets).

Tagged Photos

If you're one to flaunt your adorable pics, it's crucial to constantly screen your notifications to see who is tagging you in what. Are you scantily clad? Is there a beer can creeping in the corner of the photo? Did you go a little overboard at that theme party? Even if you're of age, you shouldn't have photos of you with alcohol in your pictures; it's better to be conservative in these situations! When it comes to jobs and internships, you don't want to introduce any doubt about your maturity, ability, or reliability to employers who are perusing your photos.

As a rule of thumb, alcohol should not be displayed, since those photos could factor into the job search process. Companies want interns who will turn into employees, and they don't want employees who they perceive will end up drinking too much with clients or coming into the office with massive hangovers. Bottom line: Un-tag inappropriate pictures or hide them entirely.

If there's a not-too-flattering video or photo of you up that isn't yours, you're going to need to speak directly with the person who owns it. Whether it's a close friend or a random peer from high school, send him a professional message explaining that you are applying for jobs and would rather the footage or photo be erased entirely. The photo owner might complain, but remind him that he too will need to go through a similar process, and owning these kinds of photos isn't looked at well by employers. Be polite but stern.

About Me (and Similar) Sections

With room for quotes, relationship status, and interests, Facebook is the social media outlet with the most room for information faux pas. It may be obvious that posting information containing bad language and drug references is a bad idea, but everything from your political views to your use of emoticons can be judged. When applying for a job, your first Facebook move should be an information overhaul. You want to come off as professional, so use your quotes and interests sections on your FB page to enhance your chances of getting a job by presenting information relevant to the job you are applying for. For instance, if you are applying for a job in the fashion industry, list fashion-related interests. But first, go through all of your information and change anything that could be considered controversial—bad language, quotes about partying, and excessive political information.

For example, let's say your Twitter bio (which is public!) has the Kate Moss quote, "My mum used to say to me, 'you can't have fun all the time,' and I used to say, 'Why not? Why the f**k can't I have fun all the time?'"

Even if it's a quote from a movie or celeb, quotes like these are inappropriate because they make potential employers worry about your character and your level of responsibility. Acceptable quotes include appropriate music lyrics, PG jokes from friends, motivational quotes, or clean quotes from celebrities.

Another thing to avoid is voicing strong political opinions in your About Me section, such as writing, "Wondering if there is anyone more insane or annoying than the Tea Party." Now, while it's okay to list political involvement like "member of College Democrats," expressing strong political sentiments is not always a good idea because the employer reading your page may either disagree with your statement or question your tact. Just like it's usually a no-no to bring up politics during a first date, the same goes for interests you portray to potential employers.

Tweet, Tweet

One of the amazing things about Twitter is that you can follow industry big names as well as your employer. Use this to your advantage: Actively "retweet" your favorite company's news and attribute them as sources on your open Twitter profile. If your employer can see that you use Twitter as a tool to stay ahead in the industry you're in, then you're golden. This shows your interest in the field and your ability to navigate the Internet in a mature manner.

Avoid using Twitter to talk about parties, praise anything illegal, or complain in the midst of tweets about your favorite company's news. All that will do is shed a bad light on you to an employer and erase the positive. If you insist on using Twitter for purely social reasons, keep it that way and make your profile private. But know that you could be missing out on a great opportunity to communicate with your employer!

Three Ways to Get the Most Out of Twitter

There's more to this social media tool than just following celebs and replying to your fave pals. Enhance your experience with these three suggestions!

1. Organize or attend a tweetup: Tweetups are actual gatherings of Twitter users offline to discuss a particular topic. Often, the tweetup will assign a specific hashtag to the event so folks who can't attend can follow the conversation in real time.

2. Live tweet: Often companies or organizations will organize a live tweet session so they can interact directly with their followers. Much like a tweetup, live tweeting is a great way for anyone who isn't present to follow the conversation.

3. Attribute sources: If you retweet (repost someone else's message), make sure you're giving credit where credit is due. This is an excellent way of building trust with your followers/readers.

Keep What Can't Be Hidden Appropriate

Even if you keep all your social media profiles private, employers can still see your main profile picture. Therefore, make your profile picture something both expressive and mature; in other words, no profile pictures of you making out with your boyfriend or double-fisting beers. Instead, make your profile a pic of you on vacation (no bathing suits!), a school photo, or a shot of you playing on your sports team—it'll seem totally normal as well as mature.

Watch Your Friends

It's often easy to forget that what other people post on your wall or tweet to you can be a reflection on you. Monitor what your friends post, because a friend saying, "we got so drunk last night" will have the same effect as you posting it. When writing your statuses, keep it clean—always.

USING SOCIAL MEDIA TO HELP YOU LAND JOBS

Your profile is clean, your job applications have been submitted—but is there anything else you can do from your computer to entice companies to hire you? Yes! It is possible to tweet your way to a job, as crazy as that seems! This approach to job hunting is becoming increasingly popular. While not everyone is able to effectively market him- or herself on the Internet, others are proving it is possible to get a foot in the door in just 140 characters.

How to Tweet with Your Employers

Start by following local companies you'd be interested in working for. Pay attention to industry happenings so you can retweet big news from your account. Include your Twitter handle on your resume, LinkedIn, and resume website (if you have one)—it shows employers that you are comfortable in that space and gives them a great place to digitally get to know you.

When interacting with the company, make it more than "hire me!" Your interactions should start before a job opening may even be available and have more depth than "hey I just sent my resume in for the marketing assistant position!"

When you turn in your resume, you get one page. When you go in for an interview, you get a small window of time. Being active on social media allows your employer to see who you are. Believe it or not, it isn't all about where you interned or where you got your degree. You'll hopefully end up spending forty hours a week with them this summer, so use Twitter to show them you're normal, you're cool, and you'd make a fun coworker.

Friending Your Internship Boss

The virtual lines between friend, Facebook friend, and coworker are hazy ones. Especially as a college student, Facebook may not necessarily be the best representation of you at your finest. While it may be tempting to friend all of your new coworkers (whether you simply want to creep on their profiles or just want to finally break that 1,000 friends mark), while you're still a student, you probably want to keep your Facebook account social instead of professional.

However, when you graduate, you can choose again to make the decision to have a social or professional Facebook (the same rules would apply to other social media applications like Instagram, too!). Then, once you decide on maintaining personal or professional social media accounts, you'll have an easy rule of thumb for accepting and ignoring friend requests.

LINKEDIN

By now, you're probably an expert at Twitter, Facebook, Instagram, etc., but LinkedIn may be the social media platform that has you a bit lost. It's a mix of social and professional—it's basically the Facebook of professional networking. It's free to use, your profile is essentially a resume, and in place of "friends," you have "connections." But it can be tricky, so keep these tips in mind to navigate the waters of the professional social network.

Personalize Your Networks

We've all been cautioned against getting too chummy with employers or professors on Facebook, and rightfully so. So when it comes time to click that little "connect" button on LinkedIn, you might feel a slight twinge of apprehension, especially if it's someone you worked with three years ago and haven't seen since. But don't be shy—this is what LinkedIn is for!

Don't just use that canned response they have: "I'd like to add you to my professional network." Personalization is key, so say something like, "We worked together during my internship last summer. Let's reconnect on LinkedIn." Making connections is the bread and butter of what LinkedIn is about. Without connections, even the most stellar of profiles will accomplish nothing. A strong group of connections is a huge resource for professional success, so don't be afraid to get networking.

Have a Completed Profile

If you wouldn't want to walk into a job interview dressed sloppily and feeling unprepared, then you wouldn't want to complete your LinkedIn profile only halfway either. This is the online equivalent of your resume, so make sure it represents the best you have to offer. LinkedIn is pretty user-friendly, with a checklist that tells you how much of your profile you've completed. So before you apply for any jobs or internships, set aside some time to tie up any loose ends on your profile. Make sure all the sections you've started are completely filled in before inviting potential employers to come take a look. You don't have to kill yourself trying to remember every single scholarship and award you've won throughout your college career, but be sure that things like job descriptions are sufficiently fleshed out.

Have a Nice, Professional Photo

The shot of you and your BFF stumbling out of the bar together may make your hair look shiny and your butt look cute, but keep it far, far away from LinkedIn. Stick with a simple, smiling portrait so that you look approachable and professional.

Keep It Relevant

A typical resume limits your list of experience, awards, and accomplishments to a single page. LinkedIn, however, has unlimited space for you to list every job you've ever had since you were a camp counselor the summer after eighth grade. It can be tempting to list all of it ("OMG look how awesome and experienced I am!"), but keeping your profile focused is key. You can take the opportunity to expand what's on your resume; if you have so many internships that they no longer fit on one page, LinkedIn is the perfect place to include them all, but as a rule, your list of accomplishments should directly reflect the type of position you're looking for now.

Utilize the Recommendations Feature

The days of cringing when you ask for a letter of recommendation are now officially over! Because LinkedIn is the "World's Largest Professional Network," it's understood that, well, networking is supposed to happen. Reach out to bosses and coworkers from past and present and ask them to put in a good word for you; having others speaking of your worth right on your profile makes you more credible.

Make Your Descriptions Accomplishment-Based and Bulleted

As if making connections wasn't stressful enough, there's still the worry that once you're connected, important people are going to be looking at your profile. Eek! Like any other potential-employer-is-reading-my-resume situation, you want the information you're presenting to (a) be easy to read and (b) show you in the best possible light.

Personalize, Personalize, Personalize!

While, yes, LinkedIn is for professionals, it's also about networking and being personable. You have the option to include links to your blog or portfolio, list your skills and specialties, and add various sections and apps to better showcase your accomplishments. If you're multilingual, add the Languages section to list your abilities. If your network spans the globe, the My Travel application will let you know when you're in the same city as a coworker. You can showcase your test scores, blog, volunteer experience, and even your reading list. The whole point of LinkedIn is to connect people; this process is greatly helped along when people feel that they can get to know you from your profile.

Contacts to Seek Out on LinkedIn

Aside from your college friends and internship supervisor, look to connect with other people on LinkedIn, such as your classmates from high school, parents' friends, friends' parents, and other interns and employees at your internship beyond just your supervisor. You never know when that connection will come in handy!

What You Should Never Do on LinkedIn

It may seem obvious what you should never write on your professional social media profile, but you'd be surprised. Definitely avoid the following, or employers will be avoiding you!

- **LOL, OMG, ROTFL:** This isn't Facebook chat, so don't use online shorthand!
- **Obvious skills:** Everyone knows how to do Internet searches and send e-mails. No need to include that on your profile.
- **Clichés in the summary:** You're given the opportunity on your profile to say a little about yourself, but using clichés and overused job-searching buzzwords and phrases like "I'm a team player" aren't really demonstrative of anything other than a lack of creativity.
- **Secrets:** If you're doing something for your employer that he or she wants on the down-low, it should remain on the down-low—not on your profile.
- **Excuses:** Don't blame anyone on your profile. If you got fired, don't mention it, and certainly don't blame someone for it on your page.
- **Lies:** Don't say you worked for a company if you never did; this will come back to haunt you!
- **Bragging:** Statements like "I'm the greatest employee in company history and am single-handedly responsible for its success" are just going to raise eyebrows and have people suspicious of you.

INTERACTING WITH YOUR FRIENDS ON SOCIAL MEDIA

Social media is a great way to share photos from your sorority crush party, stay connected with friends who are at other schools, and do a million other things. But with social media taking over our lives so much (we all know the saying, "If it's not on Facebook, it didn't happen"), sometimes it can get tricky!

Friending Before You Get on Campus

It's understandable that you're excited about your school and you want to turn to Facebook to reach out to your fellow pre-collegiettes. It's intimidating to head to a campus where you don't know anybody, so it makes sense that you want to get to know people before you arrive. Keep in mind, though, that everybody is in the same boat as you—heading to a brand-new place with very few solidified friendships or connections, if any at all. You have to strike a balance between not friending anyone (including your new roomie!) and friending everyone. You definitely do not want to be that person whom everyone remembers for her aggressive summer friending.

Avoid E-Flirting!

Just because you scoped out a cute boy whom you have begun to fantasize about with your girlfriends doesn't mean you need to post on his wall. Being flirty or inappropriate with guys you don't know will automatically give you a negative reputation. Plus, you don't even know him—he might come off completely different in person than on his carefully crafted Facebook page.

To start, reach out to students in your major or girls who have the same hobbies or interests as you. Finding people in your program or school who have common interests is a great way to connect with people you might want to be (real-life) friends with. Instead of friending every single incoming freshman you see on Facebook, friend people whom you share something with.

Another great move is to join the "Class of" Facebook groups for your specific major, dorm, or city. These groups are always fun to be a part of, as it's a cool way to interact with people you may be working, living, or studying with. This way, you're not adding everybody you don't know, but you still get a sampling of the people you may be interacting with. These groups are also great places to start a conversation with people and arrange pre-orientation local meet-ups.

Additionally, if you know people on campus through mutual friends—whether they are other pre-frosh or upperclassmen—friend them! Even if it's just your BFF's cousin's BFF, she can turn out to be a great connection, especially if she's an older student who's familiar with life on campus. Chances are if you message her politely, she'll love to answer any questions you have about campus life.

Public Displays of Social Media Affection

The social media generation has developed the ability and a subsequent need to publicize its social affairs, however explicit, dramatic, or mushy they might be. In most cases, it's just TMI. No, despite what you might think, nobody enjoys scrolling through the make-out session that PhotoBooth just happened to record.

It's great that you're in love, and even better that you're not afraid to show it. But for the sake of our imaginations, your privacy, the parents who are now starting to infiltrate the Facebook-sphere, and your potential future employers, you might want to consider not doing any of the following.

Watch What You Share

Although real problems are rare, talking to people over the Internet as a young woman can still be risky. Make sure you're not giving out things like your address or any other personal information you wouldn't want somebody you don't know to have access to. Consider cleaning up your profile and taking off any personal identifying information you shouldn't have on the Internet.

Posting Intimate Photos

It's not cute if you use the "fisheye" effect, and it's not funny with the whirly one. No one wants to scroll through your make-out album, and it's just not necessary to publish it online.

Treating Wall Posts As Love Notes

The "I love you sooOooOooOooOooOooOoo much baby" updates that pop up on Newsfeeds every twenty-six seconds are better left hand-written. Truth be told, they mean little when they appear on a computer screen, and that much less when you share those, um, deep sentiments with pretty much everyone you've ever met.

Manipulating Profile Content

Sharing usernames and passwords is one thing, but taking advantage of this valuable information is quite another. When you start posting statuses that say *"I luv my gf sooo much!!!"* and filling in his About Me section with your full name and hearts and :-*'s, it gets to be a little much. Plus, you're not fourteen anymore, so don't act like it.

Posting Super Emotional Statuses

You know, the ones that are really dramatic and vague, unless you know exactly whom it's directed towards. It's the *"Love can touch us one time and last for a lifetime. And never let go till we're gone. Love was when I loved you, one true time to hold on to, in my life we'll always go on"* updates that really get us—and drive us to text our friends to take a look. Instead of being effective, they seem overly theatrical and altogether ridiculous.

Having an On-and-Off Relationship Status

No matter how many times you break up in real life, we don't need to see that little red heart break and re-join time and time again. First of all, it's depressing, and we all feel bad for you! Second, it gets boring when you start scrolling through your News Feed and the only Top News is that "Joe Smith and Mary Lou are no longer in a relationship," and "Joe Smith and Mary Lou are now in a relationship" fourteen times. (Because News Feeds are meant to entertain, after all.)

Having Unrelated Conversations on Someone Else's Photo

It doesn't matter if it's a lover's quarrel or a little flirtation, but just remember that every time you post a comment on a picture, anyone else that has posted on it previously receives a little red notification. Your BFF Sarah doesn't want to read through the string of fifteen comments of planning for your next date, and neither do the six people that liked her picture. Pick up your phones if things are getting excessive—or X-rated, for that matter.

Wellness Check-In: Five Ways to Stay Safe on Social Media

When you're posting photos on Instagram and checking in on Facebook, it's easy to forget that social media can be dangerous at times. Here are five ways you can stay safe while using any social media application.

1. Utilize privacy and security settings on social networks to control what information people can see. If someone is threatening you, remove that person as a friend, block him or her, and report him or her. It's important to manage your friend list.

2. Think twice about everything you post on Facebook. Will a rant about your sociology class come back to haunt you one day? Press delete instead of share.

3. Keep personal info personal. Don't share your address, credit card number, social security number, or phone number online!

4. If you're uncomfortable with something, speak up. Never be afraid to ask someone to take down an incriminating photo of you. It might be awkward, but it would be a lot worse if your parents or boss saw it one day.

5. Make unique and long passwords to prevent hacking by cyberstalkers or vengeful ex-friends.

Chapter Checklist

✓ Check out your privacy settings on all your profiles so you're aware of what you're sharing.

✓ Be careful about everything you post or are tagged in. Even if you didn't post it, it still reflects on you if you're mentioned in it.

✓ Tweet at companies you're interested in, but make sure to do it in a thoughtful, mature way.

✓ Have a flourishing LinkedIn account and utilize it to connect with people who can contribute to your professional success.

✓ Don't over-friend or over-inundate other pre-collegiettes before you get on campus. Use Facebook and other social media platforms to connect with a few select students, but don't be that girl everyone already knows of (and not in a good way).

✓ Just as you should be mature about what you and your friends post about parties and letting loose, you should be mature about what you post about your relationship. No one needs to be flooded with social media PDA!

PART 5

Managing Your Money and Career

By now, you've seen that college can give you the freedom to explore new opportunities, form new friendships, and become an independent person. These four years are yours to make the most of, and we know you will! But with all this independence comes a certain level of responsibility, especially regarding managing your money and making big decisions, such as whether or not to study abroad and what kind of career you want to have. The key to anything that seems really overwhelming is preparation, and this is true for everything from your first college final to your last final-round job interview. Educating yourself on the steps you'll have to take to achieve your goals will make everything much more manageable, and you'll feel more confident in each decision you make!

In these last chapters, you'll find tips and resources to help make your new career go as smoothly as possible. We've even got you covered when it comes to making your first resume and managing your money. A career might seem daunting, but if you're proactive and plan ahead, we know you'll accomplish all of your goals and more!

CHAPTER 18

Managing Your Money

The beginning of college can be a whirlwind. Between all the parties, early-morning coffee runs, and late-night pizza binges with your suitemates, it can be easy to let something important slip through the cracks: money. From figuring out how you're paying for school to learning the art of budgeting, basic money management should start long before you get your first big-girl paycheck after college. In this chapter, we'll cover everything you need to know to become a financially savvy collegiette before you even set foot on campus!

SCHOLARSHIP SECRETS AND FINANCIAL AID FACTS

Although the value of college extends far beyond its price tag, the cost of college can still be a burden on your and your parents' wallets. After factoring tuition, room and board, textbooks, and other miscellaneous expenses into the cost of college, your dream to become a doctor or journalist can easily go from seeming possible to seeming out of your reach unless you find a way to pay for your education. But don't fear, collegiettes! There are plenty of ways you can fund your college education, and we've laid out the options for you.

Federal Financial Aid

The federal government offers grants and loans to help collegiettes pay for their college education. Your first step to getting financial aid is to fill out the Free Application for Federal Student Aid (FAFSA) (*www.fafsa.ed.gov*), which asks questions about your income, your parents' income, and your living situation to determine how much aid you qualify for and what kind of aid you'll be getting. The types of federal aid available are:

Grants

Federal grants are based on financial need and do not need to be paid back. When you apply for financial aid using the FAFSA form, you are automatically considered for government grants.

Loans

When you apply using FAFSA, you are automatically considered for government loans, which need to be repaid after you graduate or leave school. If the loan is unsubsidized, interest is tacked onto the loan as a charge for borrowing the money; if the interest is not paid while you are in school, it is added to the amount you owe and can increase your future bill when you start having to pay it back. If the loan is subsidized, that means the government is paying for the interest and you'll only have to pay back the amount of the loan, without interest, after you graduate. After you graduate, you or your parents will be responsible for paying your loans back, depending on whether you take out a student loan or a parent loan, but the government and your loan servicer (the bank that holds your loan) have several payment options to help you pay off what you owe, which you can read about on the Federal Student Aid website (*https://studentaid.ed.gov*).

Work-Study

The FAFSA form will ask you if you want to be considered for the Federal Work-Study (FWS) program. With work-study, you'll work a part-time job through your school in order to get financial aid.

Scholarships

Scholarships and grants are one of the best ways to pay for college, because you don't have to pay the money back. As long as you apply the money you receive to your school expenses, you may essentially get to attend school for free, depending on how much aid you receive.

So, where can you find them? Search online through scholarship searches and websites, and of course on your college's financial aid website. If your high school has a college resource center, consider meeting with them to discuss any scholarship opportunities unique to your school or area.

Private Loans

Private loans are taken out through your local bank. To apply for a private loan, you have to go to a bank or credit union, talk to a banker, and fill out some paperwork. Unlike federal loans, private loans require established credit, which means that your parents may have to cosign for the loan. If you've never had a credit card, this means that you don't have any credit history, and you might be unable to get a private loan without your parents' help.

How Do You Know Which Way Is Right for You?

The good news is that you can combine several methods to pay for your college education. If you have financial aid through your school and find outside scholarships, you can cover the cost of your tuition without having to pay out of pocket. Talk to your parents and your financial aid advisor to understand your college costs and your financial aid options. Then you can determine which kinds of aid you're qualified for and which kinds of aid make school the most affordable for you.

Five FAFSA Application Mistakes You Should Definitely Avoid

1. Missing deadlines: The FAFSA requires info from many family members, so make a calendar with all the due dates and start asking your family members for the necessary info well before the deadline.

2. Entering incorrect numerical information: Be very careful with any entered numbers, particularly your or your parents' social security numbers.

3. Missing signatures, either handwritten or your PIN on the FAFSA form.

4. Putting health care information in the wrong field: Be careful not to list it as untaxed income.

5. Throwing out information once you're done with it: You'll need these forms year after year, so file them away for reference!

MAKING MONEY DURING THE SCHOOL YEAR

You've figured out how best to pay for school and you're quickly settling into a routine on campus. By now, however, you might have realized that living on your own without the steady financial support of Mom and Dad can be quite pricey. Thankfully, there are tons of ways out there to make extra cash that are sure to fit seamlessly into your busy schedule—you just have to take advantage of them!

On-Campus Jobs

If you are interested in making money while in college, here are a few options to pursue:

Resident Assistant (RA)

RAs live in college housing and assume responsibility for the approximately twenty to fifty students living on their floor to create a safe and supportive environment for the students. Also worth keeping in mind: Some RAs don't receive an hourly wage. Instead, they get free housing and a meal plan. For more information about being an RA, see Chapter 11.

Peer Tutor at the Writing Center

Almost every college has a writing center and/or tutor center where students can get one-on-one tutoring at no cost. In general, tutors help with idea development, organization, and support as well as accurate source citation and overall clarity.

Teaching Assistant

If you're super passionate about a subject, field, or particular class, consider becoming a teaching assistant, or TA! TAs traditionally grade papers, lead review sessions, and hold office hours.

Library Assistant

Typical responsibilities include monitoring the front desk, answering questions, checking books in and out, helping people find books, shelving books, and answering the phone.

Off-Campus Jobs

It might be worth looking off campus for employment as well. Here are a few options you can look into to pad your bank account.

Work at a Restaurant or in Retail

Positions like these can also offer the opportunity to earn tips (in the case of restaurants) or commissions (in the case of retail). See if popular establishments in your college town are hiring! They probably love to employ local college students.

Babysit

Ask your in-state friends who live near campus if they know of any families who are in need of a qualified babysitter. Or, you could post flyers with your number on them in a professors' lounge or ask professors, administrators, and other adults you're close to if they need a babysitter or if they know anyone who could use a little extra help with their kids. You could also use a babysitting website like Sittercity or Care.com to find local families who need babysitters in your area.

Work a Part-Time Internship

Not only is a part-time internship a great thing to put on your resume, but it can also be a great way to make money. Search for paid internship opportunities in your school's area on websites such as Internships.com (*www.internships.com*) and through your college's career center.

Other Ways to Make Money at School

Hit Up a Consignment Store or Site

If you're that girl with closets and drawers overflowing with rarely worn clothing, take some of these garments to a local consignment store where you can actually get paid for those outfits that would otherwise be collecting dust. No consignment shop near your university? Check out Threadflip (*www.threadflip.com*), where you can sell your clothing online from any location, or do a search for other consignment sites.

Sell Your Textbooks

At the end of every semester, either take your textbooks to your campus bookstore or see how much you can sell them online for using websites such as Textbooks.com (*www.textbooks.com*) or Chegg (*www.chegg.com*).

Rent Out or Sell Your Supplies

Rent out or sell some of your more expensive school supplies, such as graphing calculators and clickers, to students who may need them for less than their retail price.

How to Make Time to Work and Study

While some jobs will be very flexible with your hours, others may need you to work for specific blocks of time. If you know that you'll need to get a job while at school, take this into consideration when you're building your class schedule. Your academics should of course come first, but you'll be able to dedicate more time to your classes if you aren't constantly worried about fitting in those extra shifts between lectures! Consider blocking out four-hour periods on one to two days per week so that you can ensure you'll have time to work AND time to study.

BUILDING A BUDGET

Once you've figured out how to make money while you're in school, you need to figure out how to manage this cash flow. If you've never managed your own money before, this might seem like either a daunting or trivial undertaking. In reality, it's simple and it has the potential to save you a whole lot of trouble and moolah down the line. To help you get off on the right financial foot, we've broken the college budget–planning process down into five easy steps.

Keep Track of It

In order to maintain your budget, you have to organize it and keep an eye on it. If you're a low-tech kind of gal, a spreadsheet is an easy solution—make one column for your expenses with a brief description of what they are and one for the money you're dedicating to them. You can use Excel's (or a comparable program's) calculating features to easily draw up totals and make sure that you have all of the funds you need to cover your expenditures. If you use a smartphone and want something more streamlined, there are dozens of apps at your disposal, or try a website like Mint.com (*www.mint.com*). Whichever method you choose, it'll be important to keep an eye on your budget and make sure you're not overspending.

Outline Your Expenses

While it's impossible to predict every cost you'll incur over the course of a year, there will be some definite expenses you'll need to take into consideration when charting your spending. These include things like:

- Tuition
- Housing or rent payments
- Any utility bills you're accountable for
- Food
- Public transportation, gas money, and/or trips home
- Books or other supplies your classes require (art supplies, cameras, etc.)
- Student loans

Figure out all of the things you know you'll definitely have to pay for and record their costs as accurately as possible. For expenses that fluctuate from month to month (such as utilities if you're living off campus) and expenses that you have some flexibility with (such as food, whether it be in the form of groceries or takeout), make an estimate based on the average amount you pay and give yourself a healthy margin in case you end up with a bigger bill than usual. Leaving yourself some leeway in case of those unpleasant surprises will help you avoid coming up short.

Determine Your Income

If you have a job, work out how much you expect to make per month (and don't forget to factor in those pesky, pay-eating taxes). It might vary depending on tips or what hours you're able to snag, so give it your best estimate. Plan for the minimum amount of money you could make in case it's all you get in any given month—you don't want to come up short in a delicately balanced budget. Also take a look at loans, scholarships, or any other aid you might be getting from your family or other sources.

Balance Your Budget

Once you've determined your expenditures and how much money you have to work with, figure out exactly where your money is going. The first thing you should do is line up your financial aid and any money your parents have agreed to contribute with the expenses they cancel out, whether they be housing or tuition. From there, total up the amount of money you'll need to pay out of pocket to cover the rest of your inflexible expenses.

While many collegiettes would like to think that they can limit their spending to necessities alone, the odds are slim that you'll be able to resist the lure of a girls' day out or a little shopping spree every once in a while—and understandably so. So plan to buy that perfect little black dress you'll find when you're "just looking" or splurge on a mani-pedi with your gals once in a while. Also consider things like haircuts or gifts for your friends—expenses that pop up here and there over the course of a semester. Setting aside money for emergencies is also a good idea. Laptops and phones can break, and if you've ever found yourself without one of the two, you know it's the sort of weird social experiment you don't want to suffer through. If you don't end up using the money you set aside for it, roll it over to the next month or drop it into your savings.

Another good tip if you find yourself with a lot of extra spending money: save some! It's not a bad idea to put a portion of your paycheck into your savings account if you can spare it in case an unplanned adventure pops up, like studying abroad or a summer internship away from home. Decide on a specific amount you want to save each month and make it an inflexible expense—that way you won't be tempted to dip into it when you find yourself short on shopping-trip funds.

Stick to It and Adjust Accordingly

Do a month-long trial and really try to stick to your plan so you can see if the budget you've set up is realistic. It's important to remember that your budget must be flexible enough that you can adjust it to work for you! At the end of the month, tweak your plan to better fit your spending habits. It may be a few months before you get it exactly right, but once you do you'll be glad for the spending structure instead of always getting by on your last few dollars!

How to Prepare for Hidden Costs

Your education may be priceless, but it still comes with a hefty price tag. Keep the following potential costs in mind when creating your budget:

- Supplemental books for your courses
- Study supplies (printer and ink, or Scantron sheets)
- Class fees (such as for labs and art classes)
- Living expenses (coffee, toiletries, paper goods, laundry, etc.)
- Social expenses (student organization or Greek life fees)
- Side trips and vacations (spring break and weekend trips)
- Entertainment (concerts, movies, and other activities)

Wellness Check-In: Three Money Safety Rules to Master

1. Even if you're best friends with your roommates, keep personal documents hidden or locked away, and don't ever share your financial account information, including your ATM PIN.

2. When you go out on weekends, bring only the absolute necessities. Bring cash instead of a credit card and, if possible, leave your license at home as long as you have your student ID on you. These all provide easy ways for a thief to track your identity. And, let's be honest, alcohol doesn't exactly help us keep track of our belongings, either.

3. If you receive new or replacement credit cards or documents, be sure to shred the old ones before throwing them away.

Chapter Checklist

✓ Talk with your parents about what they're able to cover financially.

✓ Meet with a college or financial advisor about different financial resources, such as scholarships, financial aid, and loans.

✓ Fill out all of the applications and make sure to proofread them! Enlist assistance as necessary, especially from your parents with the FAFSA.

✓ Do your job research and figure out what opportunities are available to you and fit with your schedule.

✓ Create a budget that outlines your expenses and income, but make sure to adjust it as necessary.

CHAPTER 19

Landing Jobs and Internships

The words "internship search" or "job search" are enough to send most collegiettes running in search of a pint of ice cream and a dark closet to hide in. We know it can be scary, but the earlier you prepare for the internship or job hunt, the better off you'll be! The process of figuring out which positions to apply for can also be very enlightening—and really, isn't one of the goals of college to figure out what you want to do? From perfecting your resume and cover letters to nailing down the perfect letter of recommendation, we know what it takes to land your dream internship or job—and we know you can do it, too! Here's how.

GET FAMILIAR WITH YOUR SCHOOL'S INTERNSHIP POLICIES

Every university and college out there has different rules for applying for internships. Internships are typically open to college students during summer, fall, winter, and spring. Many companies only accept applicants who can receive the internship for credit, especially if it's unpaid, so make sure to speak with your department advisor or dean to figure this out before you go on the hunt. Your best bet is to send him or her a friendly e-mail after the holidays inquiring. Depending on your major, you may be able to take more than one internship for credit; look out for this so you can use it to your advantage!

Soul-Search and Set Goals

Your major may give you the freedom to intern for all sorts of positions, and you don't need to intern in something related to your major if you don't want to! Explore your interests and major to pinpoint what your aspirations are. Try to focus your concentration on a specific aspect of your field, what you like about it, and what you're good at. Once you have an idea of what kind of internship you want to land, it's time to research some companies.

PHILANTHROPY AND VOLUNTEERING

Odds are you aren't new to the world of philanthropy, having done community service in high school to meet volunteer hour minimums and to fill up your college applications (and hopefully also because you like giving back to the community!). In college you'll get the same benefits, but also meet people with similar interests and hopefully find an organization that stays close to your heart long after graduation. Plus, no matter what you want to do with your life, employers will always be impressed that you used your personal time to help others.

A demonstrated interest in and passion for community service can go a long way on the job market, so you'll be doing double (even triple!) duty with those hours, as you help others, help your chances in the job market, and feel good about yourself while doing it. The specific cause you choose to get involved with isn't what matters—it's about picking a project or organization that means something to you. You'll be able to leverage that passion in interviews down the line, and how much you care will shine through when you talk about your activities because it will be truly authentic.

There is an extremely wide range of things you can get involved with philanthropically on campus; the volunteer organizations listed here represent just a small slice of the options!

Relay For Life

Relay For Life is a volunteer-driven fundraising event for the American Cancer Society that is held annually around the world. The event raises money for cancer research and cancer patients while spreading awareness, celebrating the lives of survivors, and remembering those who have lost their lives to cancer.

All Relays are overnight events lasting twelve or twenty-four hours that usually take place on a school track. Since it is a "relay," each fundraising team has to have at least one person walking the track at all times. The event consists of a variety of different ceremonies, including a special lap for cancer survivors, a survivor dinner, and a candlelight vigil.

In addition to attending the event or participating in a team, you can also meet new people by joining one of the committees that plan the event. Although Relay For Life only happens once a year, there are many team-building and fundraising activities leading up to the event. Whether you're interested in event planning, marketing, recruiting, or philanthropy work, Relay For Life offers a chance to explore your individual interests and work as part of a team to raise money for an amazing cause.

She's the First

She's the First is an organization that sponsors girls' education in low-income countries, helping them literally become "the first" in their families to graduate from a secondary school. Supporters of the charity fund scholarships and provide information to help people understand the rippling effects of poverty.

Many campuses (and high schools, too!) have independent chapters that host fundraisers such as tie-dyed cupcake campaigns and races that help them sponsor girls at She's the First partner schools. Additionally, campus chapters spread awareness and create a dialogue in their residence halls as well as on social media.

Environmental Clubs

Campus environmental clubs have a wide range of ecological goals, but promoting sustainability on campus is a popular one. Environmental campus groups use their influence to promote changes on campus to accomplish such goals as conserving energy and reducing waste.

Other groups do things such as work to educate the university about environmental law and other larger scale environmental issues, promote sustainable food systems, and expose others to movements such as veganism. If you love your school colors but your heart is truly green-leaning, these are the clubs for you.

Where to Find These Clubs

Before arriving on campus, check out the Student Life pages on your university's website to get a feel for the clubs they have on campus.

At most colleges, orientation is the time when clubs will be frantically trying to recruit incoming freshmen. Don't hesitate to check out the clubs or to talk to students in charge of the organizations during a club fair.

If your school doesn't have an orientation club fair, don't hesitate to reach out via e-mail to the club contact on your school's website. (All clubs will have a contact listed for people who want to get involved.)

CREATE A LIST OF POSSIBLE INTERNSHIPS

Searching for an internship is essentially impossible without knowing what you're looking for. Start off this process by creating a list of companies you'd love to work for. Make sure to apply to a lot of different internship programs, since most are extremely competitive. Casting a wide net—within desired industries, of course—will better your chances of snagging the one that's perfect for you. If you're not sure where to start looking, begin by searching internship websites, company websites, and your school's internship database. Who knew that surfing the web could be so productive?

RESEARCH, RESEARCH, RESEARCH!

Now that your dream internship list is created, it's time to research! But what are you supposed to look for? Here are some factors and details to consider as you map out your search:

- **Location:** Is the internship in a city that you'd like to spend the summer in?
- **Housing accommodations (if necessary):** Does the internship provide them or, if not, would they be easy to find?
- **Paid versus unpaid:** How will you be compensated?
- **Application due dates:** Are they feasible for you to meet?
- **Whether the internship will give you college credit**
- **Eligibility:** Do you meet the requirements? Just remember that every internship has different requirements.

To prevent a serious mix-up, keep all of this information organized. Create a spreadsheet or Google Doc with all your research. We promise that researching a ton and being organized will make this process less stressful.

TALK TO A CAMPUS CAREER COUNSELOR

Although you've done all the research, you might still have more questions. Luckily for you, your campus's career center has all the answers: It's there to help you snag sweet jobs and internships. With all of their knowledge, your school's career counselors will definitely be able to help you out. Plus, your career advisor may have more internship suggestions! So call your career center and set up a meeting; a scheduled meeting will ensure a lot of one-on-one time. Don't forget to bring your resume, your cover letter drafts, and your research. The more your career counselor knows about your internship search, the more she will be able to help!

Six Things Your Campus Career Center Can Do for You

You probably never knew you could head to your campus career center for all of these resources!

Put you in touch with alumni: Most colleges have online directories or groups where you can research alumni who are working in your intended field, living in your city of choice, and more.

Help you find a job or internship: Make an appointment with a career counselor to discuss what you might be interested in doing or to figure out which internships or jobs you should apply for. Most schools even have their own job or internship posting sites for their students.

Connect you with resources to fund an unpaid internship: Many schools offer internship grants, and your campus career center will have the lowdown on these. Make an appointment at your career center to discuss the application process and requirements, since these processes can be tricky to navigate.

Review your resume: A career counselor will be more than happy to review your resume one-on-one with you and answer any questions you might have! See if your career center can recommend anyone there who specializes in your specific intended career field.

Prep you for interviews: You and a career counselor can have a mock interview and practice before you head into the interview for real.

Advise you on choosing between job offers: A career counselor can go over your options with you and help you decide which opportunity best fits your goals.

How to Do a Mock Interview

Doing a mock interview is one of the best ways to practice for the real thing. It's important to make the setup as close to the real interview as possible to mimic the way the situation will actually feel. Ideally you should have someone who intimidates you or makes you somewhat nervous as the mock interviewer—maybe that's a career counselor or an upperclassman in a club you're in. Then treat it as if it were the real thing, being aware of your body language, eye contact, "ums," and handshake. Debrief at the end of the mock interview rather than "coming out of character" during it.

PERFECT (OR CREATE) YOUR RESUME

Whether you're a rising freshman or a graduating senior, you'll need a flawless resume to impress potential employers when it comes time to apply for a position. Even if you're a sophomore or junior who has a resume, you may benefit from reviewing it to make sure you haven't missed anything. If you already have a resume, make sure to update it each semester with your latest internships and extracurricular activities. After a couple of quick edits, your resume will be ready for submission (just be sure to have a friend, parent, or career counselor proofread it first!). If you're applying for internships in various fields, consider having a few resumes on file that highlight your relevant experience for each position. Just remember to name them appropriately so that you don't accidentally submit the wrong one!

Resume Tip: Don't Highlight What You Hate!

If you were once pre-med and are now a history major, it's time to take off your pre-med societies and science clubs. Same goes for skills—if you are great with a certain computer program but really hate it and don't want a job where you're responsible for working with it, remove it from your resume. It'll free up some space too.

Customize Your Cover Letter

Your cover letter should be customized for each position you apply for. The purpose of a cover letter is to communicate to an employer why you would be an asset to the company. The first paragraph of the cover letter should be a short, to-the-point explanation of why you're writing: Include the school you attend, what you are studying, the position you are applying for, and how you found out about the position. Be sure you make it clear why this is the company you want to work for. Spend a line or two explaining why you want to work for them, and then quickly address a few things in the job description that you can tie into your resume and experience. Choose your best qualities and state them clearly and efficiently in your third paragraph. Sign off with a professional salutation such as "Best" or "Sincerely" and your full name.

SUBMIT YOUR APPLICATIONS AND CROSS YOUR FINGERS

It's the moment you've been waiting for: After all of this hard work, you're finally submitting your applications. While some internship programs require you to fill out a formal application online, others require a simple e-mail with your awesome resume and cover letter attached. If you're filling out an application, make sure to read through each step carefully; you don't want a silly mistake to ruin your chances of snagging your dream internship.

Follow Up

Once you've submitted your applications, you're just supposed to sit in your dorm room and hope for the best, right? Wrong! If you haven't heard back after a while (at least a few weeks, assuming the application deadline has passed), following up via e-mail is a good way to reaffirm your interest in the internship. Make your follow-up e-mail clear and concise: State the position you applied for and date you applied, reiterate your interest in the position, and ask if there is any additional information you can provide. Keep in mind that too-frequent follow-ups could annoy a potential employer and hurt your chances; follow up no more than every two weeks.

NAIL THE INTERVIEW

You got called in for an interview—congrats, collegiette! Now that you've impressed your potential employers with your application, it's time to wow them with your interviewing skills. Put together a professional-looking outfit to wear, map out directions to the interview spot so you don't get lost (you may even want to do a trial run if you have time!), prepare some questions to have at the ready for the end of the interview, and be sure to think through why you're excited about that company and position so you know how to reply when the interviewer asks you. Stay calm and confident and you'll be golden!

Phone Interview Tips

Phone or Skype interviews are common, especially when you might be interviewing for a position in a city far away. The tips for in-person interviews still apply, but here are some additional tips. Find a quiet, comfortable place to speak; communicate your interview time to any roommates or family so they don't interrupt you; for Skype interviews, be sure to wear interview attire; organize all necessary paperwork beforehand and have your resume and cover letter handy; confirm the time zone; use the bathroom beforehand; have a glass of water nearby; relax and take your time when speaking; be energetic and confident; say thank you at the end.

Wellness Check-In: Seven Ways to Stay Healthy at Your Internship

Fast forward to next summer and you're walking the halls at your dream internship! Here are some ways to stay healthy while you master the 9-to-5.

1. Bring your own lunch.
2. Stand up and walk around at least once an hour.
3. Stretch at your desk.
4. Set a timer to remind you to drink water every thirty minutes.
5. Take the stairs.
6. Walk to work.
7. Work out on your lunch break.

Chapter Checklist

✓ Familiarize yourself with your school's internship policies.
✓ Create a list of companies you want to work for.
✓ Do your research and meet with a career counselor on campus.
✓ Personalize your resume and cover letter for each position you apply for.
✓ Follow up on a position no more than once every two weeks.
✓ Prep for and nail the interview to score your dream job!

INDEX

FROM THE AUTHORS

The three of us founded Her Campus while we were undergrads at Harvard since we realized there was so much info that college girls were *dying* to know—everything from how to land an internship to how to avoid the freshman fifteen—but there wasn't anywhere to find it. So we launched HerCampus.com to serve collegiettes in all aspects of their lives, recognizing that college is such a crucial time and that you have a unique set of needs and questions that weren't being addressed anywhere else.

We've watched Her Campus grow over the past five incredible years, and while we're totally obsessed with our website, sometimes we just like to curl up with a good book, too! So now collegiettes (like you) can get everything you need to rock college and get absolutely as much out of it as possible, all consolidated in this one book (and yes, this book *totally* counts towards your New Year's resolution to read at least one book a month)!

HC Love,

Stephanie, Annie, and Windsor, cofounders of Her Campus

ABOUT THE AUTHORS

Her Campus (HerCampus.com) is the #1 global community for college women. Written entirely by the world's top college journalists, HerCampus.com features national Style, Beauty, Health, Love, Life, Career, LGBTQ+, High School, and Real World content supplemented by local content from our campus chapters around the world. In addition, Her Campus offers the HC Study Break e-mail newsletter, the Her Campus Blogger Network, the Her Campus High School Ambassador Program, Her Conference, College Fashion Week®, the Her Campus Shop, and even more products, programming, tools, and events to fulfill our mission of serving college women across every platform.

Her Campus serves as a career-launching point for our team of college journalists. Since joining the Her Campus Team, members have been offered jobs and internships with prestigious media and marketing companies worldwide.

Founded by Stephanie Kaplan Lewis, Annie Chandler Wang, and Windsor Hanger Western while they were undergraduates at Harvard, Her Campus was a winner in Harvard College's business plan competition in 2009 and launched that same year. Want to get involved with Her Campus? Head to HerCampus .com for information on writing for Her Campus, starting or joining a Her Campus chapter at your college, interning with Her Campus, attending our events, and much more!